The New Steak

Cree LeFavour

Photography by
Penny De Los Santos

The New
Steak

Recipes for
a Range of Cuts
plus Savory Sides

TEN SPEED PRESS
Berkeley | Toronto

Ten Speed Press
PO Box 7123
Berkeley, California 94707
www.tenspeed.com

Distributed in Australia by Simon and Schuster Australia, in Canada by Ten Speed
Press Canada, in New Zealand by Southern Publishers Group, in South Africa by
Real Books, and in the United Kingdom and Europe by Publishers Group UK.

Cover and text design by Betsy Stromberg
Food and prop styling by Jennifer Martin-Wong

Library of Congress Cataloging-in-Publication Data

LeFavour, Cree.
  The new steak: recipes for a range of cuts plus savory sides / by Cree LeFavour.
    p. cm.
Summary: "A collection of fifty-five contemporary steak recipes from
American, bistro, Latin, and Asian cuisine, each accompanied by side dishes
to make a complete meal"— Provided by publisher.
  Includes bibliographical references and index.
  ISBN 978-1-58008-890-9
  1. Cookery (Beef) 2. Beef. 3. Cookery, International. 4. Menus. I. Title.
  TX749.5.B43L45 2008
  641.6'62—dc22

                                        2007038898

Printed in China
First printing, 2008

1 2 3 4 5 6 7 8 9 10 — 12 11 10 09 08

Some of the recipes in this book include raw meat or eggs. When these foods are
consumed raw, there is always the risk that bacteria, which is killed by proper cooking, may be present. For this reason, when serving these foods raw, always buy
certified salmonella-free eggs and the freshest meat and fish available from a reliable grocer, storing them in the refrigerator until they are served. Because of the
health risks associated with the consumption of bacteria that can be present in raw
eggs, meat, and fish, these foods should not be consumed by infants, small children,
pregnant women, the elderly, or any persons who may be immunocompromised.

Contents

Acknowledgments

You can tell a lot about a person by how he or she cooks an egg. My father, Bruce LeFavour, knows how to handle one like nobody else. It was one of the first things he taught me. I'd like to thank him for his patience, for his generosity, and for sharing his expansive knowledge. Most of all, I'd like to thank him for instilling in me a love of sitting for hours at table with family and friends. Without him, I wouldn't be a cook at all.

If without my dad I wouldn't be a cook, then without Dwight Garner there wouldn't be a book. This one is for you, as always. You make it all worth doing—and you wash dishes like a champion. To our kids, Penn and Harriet Garner LeFavour, thanks for putting up with steak for dinner every night for months. I love you.

Thank you to my charming and steadfast agent, David McCormick of McCormick & Williams, and to Lorena Jones at Ten Speed Press for envisioning this book. To my brilliant editor, Melissa Moore, thank you for making this a better book in every regard. Many thanks to Penny De Los Santos for bringing this food to life in your beautiful photographs. And to food stylist Jennifer Martin-Wong for your inspired work. To everyone else who contributed to this project, in particular Karen Levy, Jennifer McClain, and Betsy Stromberg, thank you.

Finally, I am grateful to the friends and family who've sat around a table with me, late into the night. You are my trusty recipe testers and the people who get me into the kitchen with my apron on: Walter Garschagen, Elizabeth Gilbert, Erin Hanley, Pat LeFavour, Nicole LeFavour, Catherine and Jonny Miles, Bill Rappel, Paula Routly, Peter Rundquist, Annette and Kemal Solokoglu, Dave Weinstein, Sid LeFavour, and Lisa Weilbacker. Special thanks to Faith Echtermeyer and Lynn Hawley, for sharing their remarkable energy and enthusiasm with me.

Introduction

"The only time to eat diet food is while you're waiting for the steak to cook."
—Julia Child

I might as well start with a confession: I'm a restaurant brat. I grew up watching great food happen. In the 1960s, '70s, and '80s—before this country's food revolution, back when everyone seemed to be pouring canned soup over everything—my father owned and cooked in three restaurants (in Aspen, in Idaho, and in California's Napa Valley) that were ahead of their time. Big-city critics raved about them. Serious eaters would climb on small airplanes just to visit. When we were in grade school, my sister and I were the freaky kids who took leftover frogs' legs to school in our lunch boxes.

You can't grow up in an environment like that without learning some things. I picked up the right way to hold a chopping knife, how to make not-bad fish stock, and how to do things like whisking together lovely, delicate sauces. If you think chefs are obsessed with fresh ingredients these days, you should have seen the funky Idaho ranch where my family raised almost everything the restaurant served. We kept chickens (fryers and layers), ducks, pigs, geese (once we even got a natural foie gras, a deliciously overgrown liver, from a very greedy goose), rabbits, dairy cows, and goats. Herbs and vegetables? Our garden was big enough to play hide-and-go-seek in.

After years of milking Emily, my fawn-colored Jersey cow, twice a day, and regularly sneaking into the walk-in cooler to steal a finger of the heady yellow cream that had risen to the top of the jar, how was I to know that food wasn't the center of everyone's universe? When the restaurant closed for the season, food *and* travel were my family's obsessions. If we weren't in Mexico seeking out the best huevos rancheros, mole, or ceviche, we were in France, biking our way from one Michelin-starred restaurant to the next. Funny how those trips were timed perfectly so that we'd always hit a hotel in a town with a three-star restaurant just in time to clean up and get changed for the long Sunday afternoon meal. Back then, before anyone else cared, my family's focus on food seemed normal. But then, just about everything about childhood seems normal until you grow up and realize it isn't.

So what can I say, I was a premature foodie. But though I learned to cook by having a world-class chef in the family, and even if I'm a bit of a dinner-party junkie who likes nothing more than playing around in the kitchen, preparing complicated meals for my friends, the stuff I cook and eat most often are fresh, delicious dishes that I can throw together in an hour or so.

Quite often, that means steak.

Growing up, I didn't eat a lot of it. It was "going out to dinner" food, because sometimes the only really good thing on a menu back then was an honest steak. I proudly ordered mine "very rare" at an age when my feet still didn't touch the floor. But it wasn't until four years ago that I got serious about cooking my own steaks; that was when, like almost everyone else I know, I jumped on the protein-happy diet bandwagon. It was great for a while. Until crusty bread and buttery pasta called me back from the brink and I happily returned to my old ways. What didn't change is that back then I ate a lot of steak and I still do. I also got pretty ambitious about preparing it. After several years of steady experimentation, I decided it was time to put all of these recipes together in one place.

I've written these recipes down the way I see a plate—as a complete entity. Because that's how I think when I'm planning dinner. I don't think: T-bone steak on the grill. I think, how about a T-bone steak cooked on the grill with some of that great balsamic vinegar I just bought. And then the vinegar reminds me of the farmers' market and the gorgeous beets with their greens I saw there . . . and then I think of the herbs in my garden and how some polenta with those chopped on top would round everything out—grounding the greens, smoothing out the steak, buffering the wine. So that's one of the reasons this book is designed the way it is, with side dishes right alongside the steak recipes.

I wrote *The New Steak* because I simply love steak and eat a lot of it. But I also wrote it because eating steak has gotten kind of complicated in recent years. For starters, beef production has been commercialized and centralized. What this means is that it's harder to find flavorful steaks from cattle who've lived long enough, and walked around enough, for their meat to develop even marbling and deep flavor. To make things worse, grocery store chains have pushed out small neighborhood butchers, making it almost impossible to find properly dry-aged steak outside of fancy big-city markets. So what I mean when I say eating steak has gotten complicated is that buying a piece of meat is no longer a simple transaction. Rather, it involves food ethics; sky-high prices; decisions about whether to buy local, organic, or grass-fed beef; and figuring out what the labels and the name on the various cuts mean. Maybe the best news is that there is very good meat available these days and, if you know where to look, a seemingly endless supply of terrific raw ingredients.

This book takes advantage of the great meat and produce out there while simplifying some of the complications. I hope this book will encourage you to go beyond the basic steakhouse preparations and explore new and unfamiliar cuts. Who can argue with a perfect porterhouse? A rib eye surrounded by a classic red wine sauce? This is steak done the way we've all come to know it—porterhouse with wild mushrooms, strip steak with Roquefort butter, filet béarnaise—I love them and you'll find them here. But there are other cuts worth knowing about, and there are fresh ways of working with them, too.

Take skirt steak. It's a long, thin cut of meat that not only is inexpensive and easy to cook but also packs more rich, beefy taste than almost any cut available. Most often used for fajitas, this is a wildly undervalued cut. Toss it with ginger, hot peppers, and fish sauce, and you'll think you've landed in Bangkok. Or take hangar steak. It's another amazing piece of meat most people don't know about—unless they happen to frequent a perfect French bistro where it's on the menu as *onglet*. In this book, you'll find it with a potent salsa verde, or ground into the best burger you've ever made. Vanilla sauce on filet with a coffee rub? Eat it with that pinot noir you've been hoarding and you may just discover your own miniature version of food nirvana.

Steak isn't fussy food, and the recipes here respect that. While details do matter, I'm an advocate of simple food. Beef has a long-standing place in simple, straight-up American cooking. So while *The New Steak* is a book for people who want to do more than throw a steak on the grill—though I will tell you how to do that, too, by the way—it's not intimidating or dogmatic. With children and dogs underfoot, my kitchen is a busy, easygoing space, with none of the stress you'll find in a professional kitchen. I hope these recipes, informed by my past as a farm girl, a foodie, and a traveler, make you want to invite some friends over, buy some great steak, and get cooking.

Steak Basics

How to Use This Book

Ideas, as much as instruction, are the currency of good cookbooks. I hope reading my recipes will get you excited about cooking steak. Use the book to gather ideas about how to put together a menu on your own. That means combining the steaks and side dishes in a way that appeals to *you*. The same goes for choosing the cuts of meat for a recipe. I hope you'll explore unfamiliar cuts and try some of the things I suggest for putting a plate together, but I realize many people already have strong ideas about what they like.

Please don't meticulously measure every little item I call for. Who measures chopped herbs? I don't. I've given the quantities, because there are people who like to know *exactly* what the recipe calls for. Writing "1 shallot, chopped" is simply too general for many people's comfort. Okay. After all, a large shallot can produce 4 tablespoons while a small one can be barely 2 tablespoons. But would it matter a great deal if you ended up putting in 2 or 4 tablespoons? The sauce would certainly taste a little different, but it wouldn't be bad in either case. So if you tend to measure and worry, the quantities are here. But I hope you'll at least consider using your own good sense. Rather than awkwardly stuffing 2 tablespoons of cilantro into a measuring spoon, just chop up what looks to be about that much and be done with it.

Portion Size

In my recipes I generally call for 8 ounces of meat per person. This is a loose guide; your steaks will always be a little over or under that amount. Plenty of thick-cut steaks weigh in at 12 ounces each. Don't worry.

However much you buy, there will be people who eat more than that 8 ounces (big, hungry adults and teenagers), and others who consume a lot less. To my mind, half a pound of meat is about right—but then, I love steak and I also like to have leftovers for steak tacos the next day.

If you're concerned about the increasingly high price of buying top-quality sustainably raised steak as well as about the ethics of eating meat, given how much energy and fuel goes into producing each pound of meat, consider cutting the portion size in half while doubling one or both of the side dishes. This is a way of thinking of the steak as equal in importance to the side dishes. Eating a little less really great meat is a smart approach to ethical consumption. Rather than buying 2 pounds of cheap supermarket sirloin, splurge on 1 pound of locally raised porterhouse or, if you can find it, a pound of grass-fed, dry-aged sirloin. Take the time to make a sauce and savor every bite.

Matching the Steak to the Recipe

Almost every recipe in this book can be made with any of the steaks listed below. If that isn't the case, I'll make note of it. Just because a recipe is called Porterhouse with Black Mexican Chocolate Sauce doesn't mean you can't use strip steak. Sure, if you're cutting up meat for fajitas or doing a wok stir-fry, it doesn't make sense to buy an expensive bone-in rib steak. Even if you did, the meat would be excellent after you cut it off the bone. Some cuts are leaner, some are thinner, and some have more flavor than others. I make it clear what my favorites are—your tastes may tend in another direction. Use what *you* like.

Know Your Cuts

It's hard not to be stumped by the endless litany of names that butchers, grocers, and cookbooks use for the same cuts of meat. We're a big country, with regional distinctions, and while a strip steak is sometimes just a strip steak, it's not always. Sometimes it's a shell steak, or an ambassador steak, or something else again.

Stepping back a bit, it helps to understand that American butchers (and the USDA) uniformly divide the cow's anatomy into eight regions. These are the primal cuts, and they matter; if you remember the names of the key primal cuts, they can guide you through the maze of marketing and gimmicks that show up in the butcher case. Usually, there is some indication of the primal cut on that package somewhere. You've probably heard the names or seen them on packages of steak or ground beef: short loin, sirloin, rib, round, chuck, flank, plate, and shank and brisket. You don't need to remember all this; just remember that the best steaks, and the most expensive steaks, are cut from the cow's loin or rib section. They include the T-bone, strip steak, porterhouse, rib eye, rib steak, and filet. If you remember these names, along with the hidden greats—skirt steak, hangar steak, flank steak, and flat iron steak—you'll have it just about covered. Where's the ubiquitous sirloin? I left it for last because, while sirloin can be very good, most people already know about it. I find the range of cuts from the sirloin tricky. If you're buying top sirloin at the supermarket, it can be wan, lean, and flavorless, while grass-fed sirloin ranges from very good to a little tough. So while you will find sirloin called for in the recipes here, be aware that you need to hunt around a little to find worthy steaks from this part of the cow.

SKIRT STEAK: The star of my steak universe, this beats pretty much any cut for flavor and ease of cooking. Skirt steak is characterized by its long shape and open, grainy texture. It's a terrific steak favored by many great chefs, and it's always a bargain. Trim any sinew or fine membrane that the butcher has not removed. Remember to keep it rare—it gets tough if you overcook it. Always slice skirt steak against the grain, creating long, thin strips. It looks different but tastes better than most of the steaks you're used to. Skirt steak is also known as Philadelphia steak, churrasco, and fajita meat.

HANGAR STEAK: As close to skirt steak in price and flavor as you'll get, this cut is thicker and a little leaner. There's only one hangar steak per animal. If you buy a whole one (about 2 pounds from a big animal), you will need to remove the tendon that runs down the center of the steak. Most butchers will do this for you, but it's easy to do yourself even if you aren't handy with a knife. (Use a sharp filet knife to gently cut the tendon out while doing as little damage to the surrounding meat as possible. You'll end up with two pieces of steak that look like slightly uneven, lopsided filets.) The giant beefy flavor and that grainy texture make this steak one of my favorites. Hangar steak is also known as flap meat (which is a misnomer), butcher steak, hanging tender, and, in French, *onglet*.

FILET: This is the most tender piece of meat you can buy and one of the most expensive. Despite its exalted reputation, it isn't my favorite. Treated right, it can be outrageously good, with a light taste and a buttery texture; left to stand on its own, it can be dull and short on flavor. Experiment with it and see what you think, but always keep it rare. It sautés up nicely in a pan because it's flat and boneless, and it takes effortlessly to a rich sauce. Filet is also known as tenderloin, chateaubriand, tournedo, and filet mignon.

PORTERHOUSE, T-BONE, and STRIP STEAK: I love these steaks from the short loin, even if they do have too many names. The T-bone contains a little of the filet, while the porterhouse contains more, often with a bone to separate the strip from the filet. The porterhouse is a nice balance between the slightly looser grain and bigger flavor of the strip alongside the tender filet. These steaks should be cut thick and visibly marbled. The very tasty strip steak comes boneless or bone-in. With the bone in, this steak is known (among other things!) as a cowboy steak—a name that makes me love it more. Strip steak is also known as top loin steak, club steak, shell steak, New York strip, Kansas City strip, ambassador steak, and hotel steak. Phew!

RIB STEAK and RIB EYE: Think prime rib and you'll get the idea. Finely grained and rich, a steak from the rib has great marbling with plenty of flavor. It's hard to beat for richness and succulence. Splurge on occasion for a prime, dry-aged rib steak with the long rib bone still attached. It's one of the sexiest steaks you can serve. The boneless version of a rib eye is also known as Delmonico steak, Spencer steak, entrecôte, and market steak.

TOP SIRLOIN: Boneless top sirloin is a very common steak that many people gravitate toward because they know it so well—this is the Merlot of beef cuts. I'd encourage exploring other cuts, even though these steaks can be excellent if you seek out nicely marbled, center-cut pieces or buy a better grade. There is a wide range of other steaks from the same primal cut, including tri-tip, top and bottom butt steaks, and sirloin tip steak. One of the better steaks with a bone is called a pin-bone sirloin. Meat from the sirloin can have a dense meatiness that is very appealing if it isn't too lean.

TOP BLADE STEAK/FLAT IRON STEAK: I don't know why I turned up my nose at this cut for so long. It's very tasty and not at all expensive, and has decent marbling and good beefy flavor. Like hangar steak, you usually need to cut out the line of gristle running down its center. Not hard. All you're doing is cutting out the center tendon (which can be a little more jagged than the hangar steak's) to create two fairly tender, rectangular steaks. I like to call this flat iron steak if only to pat the marketing genius on the back for earning his money; he really came up with a great name.

FLANK STEAK: This is a lean cut from the area right behind the plate, which is where skirt steak comes from. Flank steak often gets confused with skirt steak, but it's not at all the same thing. Flank is considerably less fatty and has a dense, long grain. It's great for those who can't (or don't want to) eat more heavily marbled cuts. This cut of meat works nicely with a marinade, which is how I usually call for it here. Flank steak is also sometimes called London broil or jiffy steak.

TOP ROUND/LONDON BROIL: This is a fairly common cut from the round (yes, I know, flank gets called London broil; I told you it was a conspiracy of confusion). If you're marinating, this cut can substitute for flank steak or top blade. Turn to it for any of the wok preparations that call for soy sauce and then get thinly sliced to cook. It can be pretty tough, so choose a different cut if you're grilling or pan-frying and serving with a sauce.

FLAP MEAT: The appearance of this cut in supermarkets is a fairly recent phenomenon. Coming from the belly of the cow, these steaks are thin and nicely marbled. Technically, they are the flap of the loin. I urge you to try them. They have good flavor and do nicely when grilled or pan-fried. Keep them rare, just as you would a skirt steak or flank steak, and slice them against the grain. Sometimes flap meat is mislabeled as sirloin tips—it's neither. Look for it labeled using the French word *bavette*. (Beware: hangar is sometimes also called *bavette*, too.)

Eating Meat

Meat eaters are responsible for seeking out—even demanding—meat that comes from cows that have led what I'll call a cow's life. I see a herd of Black Angus cows living this kind of life every day, in the pasture across the road from my house. And while they're bound for the dinner table, a cow living such a life enjoys green grass, open space, sunshine, and plenty of fresh air. The good news about ethical eating is that the best-tasting meat, with deep flavor and rich marbling, doesn't come from cattle that have been rushed to the market through the use of corn, hormones, and antibiotics. Instead, the best-tasting steaks come from cows that are at least eighteen months old; have eaten grass, weeds, and alfalfa; and have walked around, smelled the breeze, and used their legs. In short: great steaks come from cows that have lived a cow's life.

Buy the best meat you can and know where it comes from. Not only is this meat better for you, but you're also helping to support ranchers and grassy pastures. Pastureland provides more than grass—it means preserving open space and the livelihood of the people who work that land. Good steak is worthwhile on a bunch of extremely compelling levels.

Buying Steak

Read labels and ask questions before you buy steak. I can't encourage this enough. As uncomfortable as it might make you, the ethics of how our food is produced is a growing part of the decisions we make about what we eat. Beef that is raised primarily on grass in a way that is environmentally sustainable and humane is more and more available. But there's also a lot of confusion out there about the real meaning of "natural," "grass-fed," "organic," and "local," not to mention "Certified Black Angus" and terms like "Kobe style." To help you make smart choices, I've put together a brief guide to help you find your way through the mysteries of meat labeling.

Grass-Fed and All-Natural Beef

Cows are supposed to eat grass, with perhaps a little grain thrown in for dessert. Look carefully at labels. The word *natural* is a pretty meaningless term in the food industry; you need to look for the words "no added growth hormones" and "no antibiotics." Since you can't easily raise cattle on grain in cramped feedlots without antibiotics, this usually means the cow was fed primarily on grass with perhaps a brief period of corn and other grains to finish before slaughter. Meat from grass-fed cows is also higher in the good fats (omega-3 fatty acids) and lower in the bad fats (saturated fat) than meat from grain-fed, intensively raised animals. That means grass-fed steaks taste better *and* they're better for you. Now how often does that happen?

Niman Ranch, one of the first producers of natural meat, is an industry leader. Laura's Lean Beef is another large producer. I buy most of my meat at Whole Foods, which carries only beef raised without added growth hormones or antibiotics. They're all grass-fed, but the cows' diets are supplemented by grain. Some companies claim their cattle are *never* fed grain in order to produce healthier, leaner meat. One such outfit, raising Black Angus cows on pure grass in Dillon, Montana, is La Cense Beef. See the Pantry at the end of the book for tips on where to purchase grass-fed meat.

Organic Beef

Unlike the term *natural*, the word *organic* does have a legal, USDA meaning. Steak labeled organic comes from cows that have been fed certified organic grain, grass, and hay. It also means they have not been crammed full of growth hormones or regularly fed antibiotics. Grateful Harvest is one company that sells organic steaks at my grocery store. They are a little more expensive, but I feel good about eating them, and they have great flavor.

Locally Raised Beef

Local is the new organic. People are recognizing that the fossil fuels necessary to transport that organic steak to your table is as wasteful and environmentally irresponsible as the feedlots we're trying to put out of business by buying organic in the first place. Just because a local farmer hasn't had his or her land certified organic doesn't mean he or she isn't using sustainable practices. I buy locally raised steaks at my tiny farmers' market in Cold Spring, New York. It's not organic, but I know where it comes from and how flavorful the meat is. I have the added bonus of supporting local farming, eating responsibly, and enjoying the benefits of more open pasture in my community.

Certified Black Angus

This label indicates little about how a cow was raised or what it ate. Instead, the Certified Black Angus label indicates a level of marbling, the maturity of the cow, and other factors that affect the quality of the meat, as well as indicating the purity of the breed. (Cows need not be pure Black Angus to meet the qualifications.) As a consumer, I don't find this particular stamp all that useful, even if the meat is of a slightly better grade. More useful is a recent development on Certified Black Angus packaging indicating the meat is "natural" with "no added growth hormones" and "no antibiotics." Now that means something to me.

Kobe and Wagyu Beef

These are super-rich, big on flavor, tender like butter—and as expensive as a vintage Chanel suit. Just so we're clear: Kobe is a region, and Wagyu is a breed. Don't be fooled into thinking you're eating Kobe beef unless you happen to be in Nagasaki. That said, American ranchers have imported

Wagyu cattle and have had excellent success raising them in the United States on a balanced diet of grass and grain. By all means get your hands on some if you can. Snake River Farms is the best-known source for American Wagyu beef (often called Kobe *style*), but there are others. See the list in the Pantry.

USDA Grades

Almost all of the beef that's sold in this country is graded by the USDA according to the degree of marbling, or internal fat, in the meat. They also consider the age and condition of the animal. The top grade, "prime," is difficult to find and very expensive (only about 2 percent of American beef is graded prime). I sometimes buy prime, dry-aged beef from high-end butchers in New York City, and it's delicious. If it's any comfort to those who don't shop in a big city, this meat also costs almost as much as my watch. Most meat that makes it to stores is graded "choice," which is the next grade down. "Select" is another step down; I'd avoid it.

So there you are, shopping in the chilly aisles of the great American grocery store. You're on your own with shrink-wrapped meat, Styrofoam trays, and a confusing array of names. Whether the package is marked as USDA Choice or not, start by looking carefully at the meat itself. You want to seek out the pieces that have a deep red color and the nicest internal marbling. This doesn't mean going for the biggest chunk of white fat on the rim of the steak (you're going to trim most of this off, anyway). No. What you're looking for are streaks with fine lines of fat squiggling through the actual muscle—just like the spiderweb pattern in marble itself. This fat is a big part of what makes your steak taste good—and it signals a better grade of meat, whatever the official grade the steak has been given.

When you get your steak home, do one last thing: take it out of its package! Whether that means cutting open a vacuum-sealed package or taking it out of its Styrofoam tray, remove it and wrap it up in some butcher paper (or use parchment paper). This prevents it from soaking in its own juices and lets it breathe a little.

Dry Aging

Really good, properly handled steaks are dry aged. Period. Problem is, it's hard to find dry-aged steaks these days because dry aging is such an expensive proposition—not only does it require time (3 to 4 weeks) and storage space, but it also diminishes the weight of the steak. As the meat air-dries, some of its moisture evaporates, giving the steak a more intense, meaty flavor. During the process, the natural enzymes in the meat also get to work tenderizing the steak. Do seek out a prime, dry-aged steak and cook it at home if you can.

Wet Aging

Wet aging isn't really aging at all. Steaks that are wet aged are generally vacuum-packed for shipping. It's called wet aging in part because the meat can be preserved longer sealed this way than it could under normal conditions. Most people agree that wet aging doesn't do much for meat beyond preventing it from spoiling. In fact, as a general rule, soaking a steak in its own juices is the last thing you want to do to it. While dry aging removes water, concentrating the flavor of the meat, wet aging keeps the meat consistently moist, diluting the meat's flavor and inhibiting much of the busy activity of the natural enzymes. These natural enzymes are the key to dry-aged beef's intense nutty flavor and outstanding tenderness.

Frozen Steak

I usually don't like frozen meat, but a vendor at my local farmers' market sells their steaks frozen when they aren't slaughtering that week. Properly handled, they can be quite good. I see it as a compromise for supporting my local farmer. For the best results, let the steak thaw in the refrigerator for a couple of hours. After that, unwrap it, get any excess blood or juices off, and loosely wrap it in butcher paper (parchment paper works, too). Set the bundle on a plate and refrigerate until it's fully thawed. As with any steak, be sure to salt it and let it come to room temperature before cooking.

Cooking and Handling Steak

Many people wonder why the steaks they cook at home don't taste as good as the ones they eat at their favorite steakhouse. Well, the grade and quality of the meat you buy is part of the answer. But the other factor is how you handle your meat from the refrigerator, to the counter, to the stove, to the plate. What follows are the essentials for getting your steaks right—better than the steakhouse. Because the truth is, no sauce, no matter how great, will cover up a steak that's been mishandled.

Freshness, Salt, and Temperature

Look for meat that has a nice, deep cherry-red color. A little bit of brown is okay, but avoid anything that looks very light pink, gray, or dark brown (dry-aged beef is more varied in color). Don't stop there. Since color can be faked with additives, the meat should have an appealing feel (never slimy) and a clean smell. It's simple: fresh meat smells good. Yes, *good*, as in clean and appetizing.

Always take your steak out of the refrigerator and let it come to room temperature before you cook it. Unwrap it, lay it on a plate, flip it, and give both sides a generous dose of kosher salt. Don't worry—it won't dry out or go bad. There is a lot of argument over the virtues and disadvantages of early salting, but I think the increase in flavor as that top layer absorbs some of the salt outweighs the minor drawback of a little surface moisture. (See Harold McGee's fabulously geeky book, *On Food and Cooking*, on the topic of salting, if you don't believe me.) If it's a scorching afternoon in August, of course, don't let a piece of raw meat sit out on the counter for hours. But under normal circumstances, letting the meat sit salted for an hour under a towel or a sheet of plastic wrap is the best thing you can do for your steak before cooking it. Will the salt bring out a little surface moisture? Sure. That's why I suggest rubbing the steak with oil before cooking.

Grilling Options

What's not to love about grilling? It's a great excuse to stand around outside with a glass of wine or a tall icy drink of any kind, just watching the flames. In the summer, I cook outside on a large, freestanding, adjustable stone grill. This giant mortar-and-stone monster uses wood— basically, you build a campfire in it and wait for it to burn down to coals—and is big enough to handle twenty steaks at once. In the winter, I grill inside, using a Tuscan Grill that fits into my fireplace. (If you have a fireplace, you *have* to have one of these—see the Pantry for sources.)

I admit I'm pretty spoiled, cooking over a live wood fire all year round. But happily, there are a bunch of ways to cook a great steak, and in many of the recipes that follow, I'll leave it up to you to pick your favorite method. Charcoal and gas grills are more practical for most people, and they do the job of cooking a steak very nicely, too.

The key to good grilling is getting the heat right so you can sear your steak without blackening it. For charcoal and wood fires, this means building the fire well ahead so that by the time you're ready to cook you have glowing-hot coals but no leaping flames.

Whatever you have—from a simple Weber-style kettle grill to a $50,000 behemoth that not only cooks your steaks but also holds your wine collection, dispenses crushed ice, and makes blended drinks—you can use it. I know plenty of people who swear by their gas grills because they don't require a lot of forethought—all you do is pop a beer, step out onto the patio, and flick a switch. Of course, if you have a grill built into your stove, great. You'll get that hot, seared texture on the outside of your meat, with a nice juicy inside—all without putting up with the bugs, cold, or dark. But just because you have one of these, don't miss out on the irresistible thrill of cooking outdoors.

So here are your grilling options, as I see them, and a few tips for getting the heat right.

CHARCOAL GRILLS

Charcoal grills automatically impart a nice smoky grill flavor, even though they are a little more trouble than gas. If you cook over this kind of grill, buy some hardwood lump charcoal and use one of those ingenious little chimney starters to get things going. No lighter fluid is required, and the briquettes not only aren't treated, but they'll also impart a little flavor to your meat because they are, in fact, hardwood.

Get the hardwood charcoal ready to light by stuffing some loosely crumpled paper in the bottom of the chimney starter and filling the top with the charcoal. Light the paper and set on a fireproof surface (I usually set it on the grill; air circulating around it is key). After 10 minutes or so, the coals will be glowing from top to bottom. At this point, you can transfer the coals to your grill and add some new charcoal on top of them. Let any new charcoal burn down to brightly glowing coals. You never want to cook over leaping flames. To test whether your grill is hot enough, use the 3-second rule: if you can comfortably hold your hand 2 inches above the grate you'll be cooking on for 3 seconds before you have to pull it away, your fire is just right. I'm a fan of a hot fire for steak; the coals should be glowing brightly with just a hint of white ash.

GAS GRILLS

Gas is very convenient and will give your steak a nice sear and even a bit of that grill-like flavor. Preheat the grill with the cover down, aiming for a reading between 400°F and 450°F. The higher BTU gas grills will make your life easy because they get really hot—35,000 BTUs and up is solid. The cheaper, weaker models will take longer. Sear the steaks over the hottest part of the grill. Don't close the lid on them! Once you've seared both sides, turn down the heat or move them to a cooler spot to finish cooking the interior of thicker steaks. If you have a very thick steak and a weak grill, you might consider moving things along by closing the lid at this point. In general, I prefer to see the steak as it cooks. I suggest keeping the lid open as you let the steak finish cooking over moderate heat.

WOOD GRILLS

I love cooking over wood and, to be honest, it's the best way to cook most steaks. Wood gives you high heat and great flavor. With the right grill and a big wood fire burnt down to hot embers, you can control your heat by scooting the coals together or by spreading them out, as you might do to finish cooking a thick steak without burning it.

Build your fire as you would build one in your fireplace, using old newspapers, kindling, and wood. Always use hardwood—pine and fir are not suitable for cooking. Fruit and nut woods, maple, hickory, mesquite—even vine clippings from vineyards—are great and will impart their own distinctive flavor to the meat. Ask around. Whatever you use, light the wood and enjoy the fire for at least an hour before you cook over it. How long it takes to get past the flames and smoke stage to the very hot coal stage depends entirely on how big your pieces of wood are, what kind it is, how well cured it is, and even on the weather. So relax and enjoy the fire. If, when you're ready to cook, you've still got one log that's flaming and smoking, just shove it aside with some tongs and settle the rest of your fire toward the back of the grill to cook your steak.

Cooking Meat on a Grill

Start with salted meat at room temperature. Check that your grill is clean and oiled—if you trim any big chunks of fat from your steak, you can use tongs to run one of these over the grill. Or use a brush with some bacon fat or peanut oil. Second, double-check your grill temperature using the 3-second rule: it's ready if you can comfortably hold your hand 2 inches above the grate—but for no more than 3 seconds. If you can do this, but only just, you've got good heat for cooking. When you put your steak on the hottest part of the fire, you should hear it sizzle. What you want to achieve now is the brown, crispy exterior that's crucial to the meat's taste, even if you like it very rare (there's serious science behind caramelized meat, but I won't bore you with it). Skirt steak, flank steak, or any steak less than ³/4 inch thick doesn't take long before it's done. The browning of the steak *is* the cooking. For these thin cuts, cook for 3 minutes or so on the first side, flip, go another 2 to 3 minutes, and then it's off to the warming oven (170°F to rest for 5 minutes). For thicker steaks, I like to sear each side and then move the meat to a slightly cooler spot on the grill to finish it up. If you have a smaller grill, you can scoot the coals aside, and for a gas grill, turn the heat way down and let the steak cook the rest of the way on the residual heat. Don't blacken your meat!

Pan-Frying a Steak

If you don't have a grill of any kind, or even a fire escape to put one on (when I was younger and lived in Manhattan's Greenwich Village, I loved my tipsy little grill set out on my fire escape amid the basil, morning glories, and straggly tomato plants), then pan-fry your steak in a little oil.

Why do I sometimes like to pan-fry my steak when I could grill it? Because, although you may get a bit of smoke in the kitchen (cooking a thicker steak like a hangar steak or a T-bone may even set off your smoke alarm, unless you have a professional vent over your stove), it's one of the best ways to control the cooking temperature while retaining the meat's flavorful juices.

Use a heavy pan—cast-iron is the best. I *really* don't like nonstick, and I don't like flimsy metal pans. If you cook a steak on your stovetop, you need a heavy pan that retains heat while distributing it evenly so one part of your steak doesn't burn while the other stays pink and rare.

Heat 1 to 2 tablespoons of peanut oil or bacon fat in a heavy pan until it's very hot—almost smoking. If you prefer butter, which is great for skirt steak because it cooks so quickly, it should be beginning to brown around the edges. Put your steak in the pan, allowing plenty of room if you're cooking more than one (the steaks shouldn't be touching). You don't want to steam the meat, and if you crowd it, you risk doing just this. Work in two batches or fire up two pans if you have to. The meat should be sizzling nicely and soon it'll begin to smoke. Flip the steak after 3 minutes and cook for another 2 to 3 minutes on the other side. Again, avoid blackening.

Go for a deep brown, crusty exterior. For thinner steaks, that should be all the cooking you need to do, and then they can go off to the warming oven (170°F). For steaks more than an inch thick, you'll need to get some heat to the center without burning the outside. For really thick steaks (1¹/2 inches and up), I like to do this by transferring the steaks, right in that heavy pan, to a 400°F oven. This is an easy method for cooking a fat steak through without filling the house with quite so much smoke. Be careful. You'll be amazed at how fast a steak can overcook this way. Check it often using a meat thermometer, and the minute it reaches between 120° and 130°F, get it out of there. If you have a proper kitchen vent, you can keep the steak on the stovetop, but you should turn the heat down. Burning the exterior overcooks the layer just beneath it, turning it gray. Instead, try to brown the outside and gently heat the inside to pink perfection.

OIL FOR PAN-FRYING

I call for peanut oil in my recipes because I like the taste and it has a high smoke point. Bacon fat is even better. I try to keep a little ramekin of it on my stove just for this reason—it's also great for greasing the pancake griddle. Vegetable oil is fine for cooking steaks, too, if that's what you're used to. Harder to find is grapeseed oil. It's a good, clean-tasting oil with a very high smoke point. Problem is, it goes rancid quickly. If you can, buy fresh grapeseed oil, keep it in the refrigerator, and use it often. And finally, my favorite fat: butter. It works okay for thinner steaks, but for thicker steaks it'll smoke and burn. You can clarify butter to give it a higher smoke point. I'm usually too rushed or lazy to do this, though.

MAKING "PAN SAUCE"

Why not use the pan you cooked the steak in to make your sauce? Sometimes you can, but often there are burned bits in the bottom that will give your sauce an off flavor. That's why, more often than not, I suggest making sauce in a separate pan with rich stock. It's a bit of a trade-off since there *is* flavor in that pan—but a burned pan ruins a sauce. My advice here is a way of playing it safe.

The Broiler

I don't love broilers. I like to be able to see and touch my food as it cooks. But if you happen to have a professional-quality broiler, great. It'll do a beautiful job of searing your steak under intense heat. In fact, that's how most steakhouses do it. But for most mortals, our ovens have so-so broilers, poor substitutes for the real thing.

If you have a good broiler, preheat it to 450°F. Be very careful, with a powerful unit, not to blacken or overcook your meat. The broiler does a nice job searing a steak, but its heat can be too intense to cook a thick steak through without burning it. Transfer it to a hot oven to finish at 400°F, and test frequently with a meat thermometer.

Judging When It's Done

The two most common mistakes people make when they cook steak at home are (1) overcooking and (2) failing to let the meat rest after it comes off the heat. Unfortunately, I can't tell you *exactly* how long to cook your steak because there are too many variables, from the thickness of the meat, to air temperature, to the intensity of your heat source. The cooking times in the recipes are meant to serve as a loose guide. You'll have to learn for yourelf how to judge when a steak is done.

Meat thermometers are great for thick steaks, and I encourage you to get one. A reading between 120° and 130°F will produce steaks that are between rare and medium-rare after 5 minutes of resting. I like to use the finger-poke test to tell when my steak is done—squishy with lots of give means very rare, while a firm steak means overcooked meat. This method, I have to admit, takes some practice. But it's pretty reliable once you get the hang of it. Make a habit of poking your meat at various stages and you'll learn the feel of a perfectly cooked steak. Of course, there's nothing wrong with cutting into your meat to peek at how done it is. I call this the nick-and-peek method, and it's one of the most foolproof methods out there. Even so, bear in mind that the steak keeps cooking as it rests!

RARE AND VERY RARE

I'm a rare and, depending on the steak, a very rare steak eater. If you're like me, you just hate to see a steak that's lost its texture and give to the heat. I prefer mine with just a little heat on the red center, a nicely browned exterior, and a soft texture.

To achieve this, aim for between 120° and 125°F on an instant-read thermometer and for no more than a hot char on each side for thinner cuts like skirt steak and flank steak. I've certainly taken steaks off the heat and rested them when they're 115°F, but sometimes they're even a little too rare for me—blue, that is. If your steak comes off the grill and turns out like this, there's nothing wrong with putting it back on the heat or in a hot oven to finish it up. Of course, there's no going back once you've overcooked a lovely piece of meat.

If you do like your steak a little more done, get there the slow way by browning it nicely over high heat on both sides and then moving it to a much less intense heat source so it can cook through. You don't want the interior to reach the high temperatures that will give it that depressing gray look just beneath the surface.

When you do decide to take the meat off the heat, keep in mind that the steak keeps cooking for several minutes, gaining as much as another 5°F on its internal temperature reading. So, even if you like your steak medium or medium-rare, the maximum temperature your steak should be at the center when you take it off the grill is 130°F. That means by the time it's ready for the table, 5 minutes later, it's going to register 135°F, which is a comfortably pink medium, but by no stretch rare.

There's a fair amount of information floating around out there that would have you think that grass-fed meat requires much more careful cooking than regular meat does. I don't buy it. The logic is that this meat is leaner than commercially raised beef, which means that it will dry out if you cook it over very high heat or cook it for too long. Okay. No doubt if you cook it for too long over high heat it'll dry out. But that's true of any steak. The truth is, I don't find grass-fed beef all that lean, and cooking any steak for too long over very high heat is a bad idea. Look at your meat. See how well marbled it is. I've seen supermarket strip steaks with next to no marbling and grass-fed strip steaks that look like Wagyu beef. It all depends on the age of the cow, its breed, how much exercise the animal got, and how much, if any, grain it was fed. Grass-fed doesn't usually mean grain-free. Buy good meat and cook it carefully, whatever the label says.

Letting Your Steaks Rest

About that warming oven. However you cook your steak, it isn't over until you've let it rest for 3 to 5 minutes in a warming oven set at 170°F or on a warm plate under a *loose* tent of foil. As the meat relaxes, it also continues to cook, so remember to account for this as part of the cooking process when you're judging when to take it off the heat. This is not some fussy, optional step. Time in a warm oven gives the exterior heat from the pan or fire a chance to penetrate the meat, melting any fat in the rare center to the consistency of soft butter.

Kitchen Essentials

Below is a list of some of the staple foods, gadgets, and kitchen habits that make cooking easier *and* better, whether you're putting together a spicy stir-fry, a rich cream sauce, or a platter of tacos. Simple things in a kitchen—good salt, warm plates, great stock—matter. See the Pantry at the back of the book for sources and tips on buying hard-to-find items listed here.

WARM PLATES

Warm plates are one of the keys to great food, no matter what you're eating. Why? Because nobody likes cold food, and a cold plate turns hot food cold in no time. Heat your plates in a 170°F oven. That way, you'll have the oven ready for resting your steaks after they cook.

ON THE TABLE

If I'm cooking a bistro- or American-style steak, and I'm not grilling my bread, I like to have a great baguette on hand. I put it on the table whole and let people pass it around—ripping pieces off as needed. Unsalted butter, served cold, is best with this—and the bread should never be hot. For Asian-style steak, rice takes the place of bread, and for Latin-style steak, warm tortillas are very inviting, wrapped up in an immaculate dish towel.

Coarse salt (I like Maldon) and a pepper grinder should be on the table for any meal. And hot sauces, in the style of the food you're cooking, should also be out. On my table, that means Sriracha with Asian food and Marie Sharp's and Lottie's for Latin food.

Finally, a pitcher of pure water, with floating rounds of lemon, crushed mint, or cucumber, is always welcome. You don't always need bubbles in your water if it has a little something else going on.

TWO GRADES OF TERRIFIC OLIVE OIL

Why do you need two kinds of good olive oil?

You need one bottle of very fresh, extra virgin, expeller-pressed oil for rubbing on steaks before they go on the grill, for pasta, and for all kinds of vegetables and sauces you don't want to overpower with too much flavor. This should be very good oil. Your second bottle of olive oil is for when you do want that big, fruity, green flavor. It's unfiltered and estate bottled, making it twice as expensive as the first, and much more intense—I'd even call it powerful. Reserve it for when you want to add serious flavor—such as on Steak Florentine (page 112), fresh mozzarella, or Fingerling Potatoes (page 140).

Once you've moved on to really good olive oil there's no going back. Inferior oils—like most of the ones on the shelf at the grocery store—have little flavor and often taste slightly rancid or musty. I don't think I'm being a snob when I say you need to look beyond the grocery store—unless you shop in an *amazing* store. It'll make a big difference in your food, I promise. I've listed some sources for buying oil in the Pantry.

CHICKEN JUICES FOR MAKING SAUCES

The best stuff to use for making sauces—by far—are the juices from a pan-roasted chicken. No kidding. Roast a big, naturally raised bird once in a while and collect all the grease, juice, and bits that end up in the pan (be sure to carve the bird in the pan). Is there a lot of fat with it? Sure, and that fat can be a delicious part of any good sauce if you choose to use it. Put the drippings in a glass jar with a lid. The fat will rise to the top and protect the precious, flavorful essence beneath. You can stick this in the freezer, using it for sauces as needed.

In case you're wondering why I'm such an advocate of chicken juices for steak sauces, I'll admit I'm generally not a big fan of beef stock, which I find heavy and less than delicious. Making your own base for a sauce takes time and planning. But like a lot of things, after you do it once, you realize just how easy it is.

To get yourself a jar of chicken juices, bring a whole, naturally raised chicken to room temperature (3 to 6 pounds is good; the bigger the bird, the more stock it'll yield). Generously sprinkle kosher salt on the chicken inside and out and stuff some herbs, if you have them, in its cavity. Cook the bird in a roasting pan for an hour or more (depending on size) at 400°F. Check for doneness by cutting into the thigh. If the juices run clear and the meat has just the faintest blush of pink, the chicken is done. Allow the cooked chicken to rest on the counter for 10 minutes before cutting it into pieces. Do the cutting while the bird is still in the roasting pan. (You could squeeze it or press on it to get more juice out, but there's really no need.) When the pan has cooled completely, remove the carcass, allowing any remaining juices to drip from it. Scrape any browned bits from the bottom of the pan and put them, along with the juices and fat, into a glass jar. Cover tightly and freeze. This yields about 1 cup.

SPICES

I often call for whole spices to be toasted and then ground. I know this is extra work, but it makes a difference. It took me forever to start grinding my own cumin, but after the first time I did it, I threw out the preground jar in the pantry. As with most foods, freshness is the key to flavor and fragrance—buy the smallest quantity you can find and throw out any spices that are more than a year old.

To toast your own spices, heat a small cast-iron pan over medium heat, then add the spices. I find that if the pan is hot, the spices take just a minute or two before you start to smell them. When that happens, they're done. Dump them onto a plate or right into the mortar for grinding.

MEAT THERMOMETER

No apologies for technology here; this is one of its benefits. Unless you plan to cook nothing but skirt steak and flank steak, which are too thin for a thermometer, you really can use one of these to guide you as you cook your big, expensive rib steaks, strip steaks, and porterhouses to perfection.

FOOD PROCESSOR

I'm not a gadget freak, but I use a food processor pretty often. Mine happens to be a Cuisinart, a brand that has pretty much cornered the market in this area. Purists hate food processors because they can eliminate variation and texture. Okay. That can happen. But the truth is, if you're careful, these machines save a lot of time, turning out perfect purees and shredded vegetables with the press of a button. If you don't have one, a blender will usually puree a sauce, and you can always use a box shredder for your slaw and zucchini pancakes.

MORTAR AND PESTLE OR MOLCAJETE

If the food processor is the Rachael Ray of my kitchen, the mortar and pestle is the Alice Waters. This indispensable item slowly but easily transforms whole spices, nuts, and herbs into more edible forms. Whether you're grinding seeds, making a spice paste, or whipping up a salsa verde, this very old-fashioned gadget will see you through this book.

ONE GREAT KNIFE

If I could choose only one knife to take with me on vacation to an ill-equipped rental house, it would unquestionably be my ever-versatile santoku. With its ultrahard scalloped edge, it can trim a steak, slice an onion, and even mince a shallot. Sure, I need a good filet knife to attack that hangar steak, and I'd hate to be without my big chopping knife if I have a lot of onions to move through. But there's no question that the knife that spends the least amount of time on the knife rack is the santoku. Keep your knives sharp or they won't do you much good, no matter how great they are.

CAST-IRON FRYING PAN

Nothing browns a steak like a simple, homely cast-iron pan. Sure, cast-iron looks prettier when Le Creuset coats it with candy-apple-colored enamel, but as versatile as these pans are, they never get that lovely patina that is reminiscent of past meals. Plain, camp-style cast-iron pans are inexpensive but conduct and retain heat much better than expensive pans do. They're easy to clean (once they're seasoned, a little hot water and a bit of mild soap aren't a big deal, whatever the purists might say). If you hate cast-iron, at least go in for a hefty pan without a nonstick coating. The hard-to-kill All-Clad pans are terrific.

KOSHER SALT FOR COOKING AND MALDON SALT FOR THE TABLE

Kosher salt is coarse but even grained and cheap enough to cast with abandon across 2 pounds of raw meat or by the handful into boiling water. I use it for everything with the exception of the final salting before food goes to the table. That's when I break out the British Maldon, with its big, jagged, uneven flakes. It adds texture and a burst of delectable brine to everything. As a bonus, Maldon is very pretty to look at if you put it in a little colored bowl on the table for pinching.

Beware: If you're using regular, fine-grain salt, not kosher, you'll need to use less of it. Kosher salt is coarser and, measure for measure, will deliver less salt to your food per teaspoon than fine table salt.

BASIC CHICKEN STOCK

Make your own stock. It's one of those things every cookbook tells you to do, but not enough people actually do it. That's partly why I've included a recipe here for the roast chicken that—without much fuss—produces what passes for *demi-glace*, the highly reduced stock that's so crucial to making a rich sauce (see Chicken Juices for Making Sauces, page 22).

For things other than a sauce, such as risotto, homemade is best—but the kind in the carton works, too. Avoid canned stocks, which can have a metallic taste. When buying stock in a carton, look at the label. There should be no MSG (monosodium glutamate) or yeast extract listed. These also give stock a distinctive aftertaste.

If you want to make your own, this is how I do it. I've approached the recipe by listing *all* the terrific things you could put in your stock. But if you've forgotten to buy celery root or don't have a parsnip, it isn't a big deal. Your stock will still taste good. The same goes for chicken parts. I like to use feet, which gives the stock body, along with wings and thighs. But use whatever you have. Breasts don't make much sense; boney parts, including the body, legs, and necks, do. And remember: don't salt your stock—salt the food you use it in.

3 stalks celery	2 leeks
1 fennel bulb, with fronds	3 carrots, peeled
1 turnip, peeled	1 parsnip, peeled
1/2 celery root, peeled	5 to 6 pounds chicken parts
5 big sprigs of parsley	3 sprigs of thyme
1 bay leaf	5 whole black pepper berries
1 star anise	1 whole clove

Cut the celery, leeks, fennel, carrots, turnip, parsnip, and celery root into crude chunks. Put them in a large stockpot along with the chicken parts. Add the parsley, thyme, bay leaf, pepper berries, star anise, and clove. Add enough cold water to easily cover all the ingredients in the pot, and bring to a boil over medium heat. Once the liquid comes to a boil, turn down the heat and skim off any impurities that rise to the surface. After skimming, let the stock simmer gently, over medium-low heat, for an hour, skimming occasionally as needed.

I don't like to cook stock for too long. Overcooked chicken has a distinctive flavor—and it's not a good one. Pour the stock through a wire sieve or a colander (you'll have a few small bits of herbs if you use a colander). The stock is done, but if you want it to be more intense or want to reduce its volume for storage, return it to the pot and simmer. Let the stock cool most of the way on the counter before refrigerating or freezing. Ice cube trays are a terrible way to store stock—they expose it to every off flavor in the freezer. A container with a tight-fitting lid works better. Leave the fat—even if you don't want to use it, it protects the stock.

CUTTING BOARDS

Wood beats plastic or silicone cutting boards. And research increasingly shows (surprise, surprise!) that wood is the safest choice when it comes to the dangers of lurking bacteria.

HOT PEPPERS

It's worth having at least passing knowledge of the Scoville scale, even if individual peppers vary so widely in how much heat they deliver. The scale is a way of measuring how much capsaicin a particular chile pepper contains. A red bell pepper has a rating of zero on this scale, while the Naga Jolokia can rate almost to a million. I like the serrano; it's hot, but not dangerous. The jalapeño, which I often call for, is mild enough to handle without gloves. They are both midrange on the Scoville scale.

BUTTER

Good butter makes a big difference. Cultured butter has a richer, more complex flavor than uncultured butter, and European butter tends to have a higher ratio of butterfat solids. If you buy high-quality butter but store it uncovered in the refrigerator, it won't taste good for long. Part of what makes butter great to cook with also makes it absorb every flavor—good and bad—in your refrigerator. Tightly wrap butter in foil to refrigerate.

One of the best butters I've ever tasted is made from the cream left over after making Parmigiano-Reggiano. Those spoiled Italian cows make amazing cream! Snatch some up if you ever see it.

MICROPLANE GRATERS

These things are amazing. They come sharp and stay sharp, delivering fine zest without the bitter pith. I also like the Microplane made for effortlessly grating fine curls of Parmigiano-Reggiano. And it does a great job on fresh ginger, too. They're available at any decent kitchen store.

A WOK

Cast-iron woks are beautiful objects. Buy a good one (see sources in the Pantry), cure it properly, keep it oiled, and you'll have it around to leave to your kids. I love my northern Chinese "pow" style, single-handled wok. Whatever you do, keep it simple. Enamel coatings, stainless steel, and all the other fancy things manufacturers do to woks only make them more expensive and less durable. Stick to the basics and wait for that wonderful patina to develop—it's like an indelible memory of all the great stuff that's been on your plate.

HOT SAUCE

There are many kinds of hot sauce out there. The distinguishing feature of a good one is a complex heat without too much acidity. Many hot sauces taste too vinegary, which can spoil anything from a taco to a stir-fry. I'm a big fan of the popular Sriracha for Asian food. For Latin flavors, I prefer a habanero sauce like Lottie's from Texas or the milder but very good Marie Sharp's from Belize.

VINEGAR

Good vinegar is as important—almost—as good olive oil. It frequently shows up in recipes for sauces where an acidic tablespoon or two adds balance. Using really good vinegar can also add complexity and depth to a sauce or a salad. Cheap vinegar tastes tinny and harsh.

There are many vinegars out there. The ones you hear about most often are made from either red or white wine. Taste and compare to find a brand you like. Other important vinegars are balsamic, champagne, and sherry. Each one will vary widely in taste, price, and quality depending on its age and origin. Balsamic is the sweetest of the three, champagne is the lightest, and sherry is perhaps the richest and most versatile. Don't overlook the more humble apple cider vinegar. Unfiltered and rugged, with a note of the apple it's made from, it's the best for making coleslaw.

RAW SUGAR

I call for raw sugar (not to be confused with brown sugar) whenever I need to add a hint of sweetness to a sauce or rub. I prefer it to the more refined white crystals of standard sugar because it has a more complex, toffeelike flavor. This flavor comes from the sugar cane juice that remains on the crystals after the initial processing. Raw sugar is coarser than standard white table sugar and measures accordingly; use a little less sugar if you're substituting white table sugar or, even better, use brown sugar. Raw sugar is widely available from a range of sources. Variations of raw sugar include Demerara, Muscovada, Turbinado, and Barbados—any of these will do—as will anything labeled plain raw sugar.

CHAPTER ONE

American Steak

This chapter is where you'll find recipes that take advantage of the produce local farmers are selling in markets all over the country—figs, olives, horseradish, cherries, watercress, and chives. The selection of produce in this country, despite the occasional shot put–worthy tomato or leathery parsley, has never been better. From Hangar Steak with French Feta, Salsa Verde, and Mint-Zucchini Pancakes (page 56) to T-Bone with Fava Beans, Purple Potatoes, Ramps, and Crispy Slab Bacon (page 48), this chapter is about straightforward methods and combinations that are bright, lively, and sometimes surprising.

The recipes here aren't complex, and the flavors come through on their own. The cleaner and more simple the food, the more crucial the quality of every ingredient. The most important pantry staples for this chapter are *great* olive oil and some chicken juices (page 22). It's also crucial to have a store nearby to supply you with fresh items such as endive, fingerling potatoes, fennel, wild mushrooms, and all those herbs. And, of course, a great butcher.

Nibbles, Starters, and Sweets

I like to stand around with a drink and some snacks before dinner. But before a big meal, I keep the snacking light. Setting out some olives (the French Luques and dry-cured are two of my favorites) or simply some trimmed radishes with soft, sweet butter and Maldon salt for dipping is often enough. For something a bit more substantial, Lemon-Artichoke Tapenade (page 62) is great on toast or crackers. For a first course, I often make a composed salad—that is, a salad with lettuce and plenty of other goodies in it, such as cheeses like French feta or blue, and vegetables and fruits like pears, apples, kohlrabi, and fennel.

Of course, all this restraint can't last. Even after a meal of steak and sides I always want dessert. There's a huge array of choices to wind up the kinds of meals in this chapter. *Good* chocolate, broken up in bits and put out in a pretty dish might be all you need—particularly if you've got some espresso and port on hand. I'm a baker and a sweet hound, so usually I can't resist putting together something more involved. It might be a fruit tart if there are gorgeous berries or peaches around or, in winter, a nut tart with a little cognac mixed in to warm it up.

Drinks

Red wine and steak make a classic pair. Whatever wine you choose, what's important is finding something that both improves the food and improves with the food. In other words, the wine should come alive and taste better when you eat it with your steak, just as the steak should suddenly gain new depth and flavor when you follow a bite of steak with a sip of that wine. It's all about what tastes good to *you*.

Cabernet is the wine—and the grape—that most people think of first for steak. It's a little more hefty and astringent than other reds, which means it can complement and be complemented by rich, red meat. Too bad cabernets tend to age so well, making these wines more expensive. So don't get hung up on cabernet. There are lots of wines, from all over the world, that work beautifully with the steaks, sauces, and sides in this chapter. Explore syrahs, petit syrahs, zinfandels, blends, and even the unjustly maligned Merlots that fill racks everywhere. Think about how rich, or acidic, or spicy the sauce is, and go from there, using your own experience and taste as a guide.

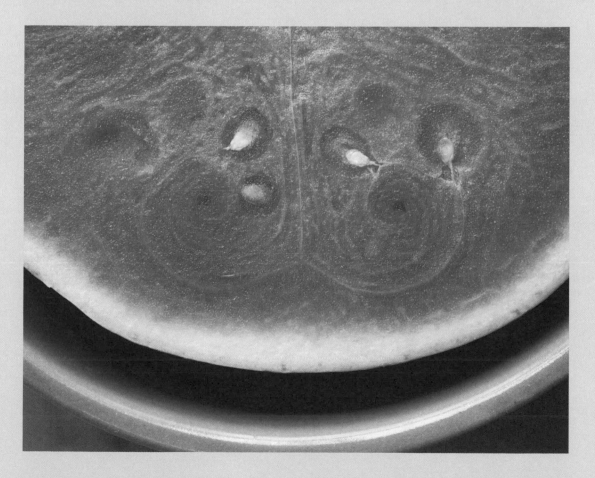

Skirt Steak Straight Up:
Hot Pepper and Pickled Red Onions with Summer Succotash and Watermelon–Goat Cheese Salad

The first time I ate skirt steak, this is how it was prepared. Wow, was I surprised. The piquancy of the onions bathed in vinegar alongside the spicy, peppery meat made me a convert to both. Don't worry if you aren't a fan of raw onions—I'm not either. The thin onions cook slightly when you pour the boiling vinegar solution over them, giving the whole mix an unexpectedly mellow quality. The succotash and the Watermelon–Goat Cheese Salad make for a lovely, fresh plate.

Serves 4

GRILL OR PAN-FRY

2 pounds skirt steak

1 to 2 tablespoons red pepper flakes

1 teaspoon kosher salt

Olive oil for rubbing

1 to 2 tablespoons peanut oil for pan-frying

PICKLED ONIONS

1 large red onion

$1/3$ cup water

$1/2$ cup red wine vinegar

1 tablespoon raw sugar (see page 29)

1 tablespoon whole coriander

2 tablespoons olive oil

Prepare the steaks by sprinkling on the red pepper flakes and then generously salting them. Let them come to room temperature, then rub with olive oil just before cooking.

For the pickled onions, peel and then slice the onion as thin as possible—what you want are nice, big, translucent circles. Use a freshly sharpened knife. Put the sliced onions in a bowl.

Combine the water, vinegar, and sugar in a pot over medium heat. Bring the mixture to a boil and pour over the raw onions. Next, using a mortar and pestle or spice grinder, crush the coriander and add it, along with the olive oil, to the onions.

Let the onions cool, and drain just before using. (Reserve the liquid; you'll want to keep any leftover onions in it to use on a cold steak sandwich the next day.)

To grill, your coals should be so hot that you can comfortably keep your hand 2 inches above the grate for 3 seconds—just! (For gas grills, this means 450°F.) Put the oiled steaks on the hottest part of the grill and sear for 3 minutes on each side over high heat. If the fire is truly hot, the steak should be cooked. If not, cook for another 2 to 5 minutes over lower heat—skirt steak should always be rare! **To pan-fry,** heat the peanut oil in a heavy pan until it's very hot—almost smoking. Sear the steaks for 3 minutes on each side over high heat. Skirt steak cooks fast— the meat should be done. If it needs a bit more time, cook for at most 2 to 5 minutes more, turning often as the steaks brown.

However you cook your steaks, check for doneness often, using the finger-poke or the nick-and-peek method (see page 19). After cooking, rest the steaks in a warming oven (170°F) or on a warm plate under a loose tent of foil for 5 minutes. Before serving, give them a final pinch of salt.

To serve, slice the meat the long way against the grain (cutting up and down the meat's length, not across it), creating long, thin slices. I like to put a few rounds of onion on top of the meat on each plate and then put any that are left in a white bowl on the table—not only are they delicious, but they're also very pretty. I usually serve the Succotash on the same plate. The Watermelon–Goat Cheese Salad is best served on a side plate.

Summer Succotash

Fresh lima beans, like fava beans, have a pod and a shell to peel. First shuck the beans, then cook them for 1 minute in a pot of boiling water. Drain and rinse with cold water before peeling off the outer shell. If you can't find fresh lima beans, use frozen lima beans or substitute edamame or another shell bean. If you're using frozen beans of any kind, blanche them first by immersing them in boiling water for 1 minute.

If you can't get the curly tops of the garlic plant called green garlic, substitute 3 scallions, with the white and a little of the green cut into rounds. For a hint of smoky flavor, grill the corn on the cob first, then shave it and add it to the pan at the last minute.

2 tablespoons unsalted butter

3 cups fresh corn kernels shaved off the cob (4 to 5 ears)

3 finger-size baby squash or zucchini, sliced into thin rounds

1 cup shelled lima beans

3 stalks green garlic, tips trimmed, chopped

1 tablespoon chopped basil

1 tablespoon chopped oregano

1 tablespoon fruity olive oil

1 teaspoon kosher salt

Freshly ground black pepper

Juice of 1/2 lemon (2 tablespoons)

In a large sauté pan over medium heat, melt the butter. Add the corn, squash, lima beans, green garlic, basil, and oregano to the pan and cook for 5 minutes, stirring frequently. To finish, add the olive oil, salt, and a generous grind of black pepper. Stir and taste. Adjust the salt as needed. Transfer the vegetables to a serving bowl and squeeze on the lemon juice just before serving.

Watermelon–Goat Cheese Salad

This salad is an unlikely combination. Once you try it, though, you'll wonder where it's been all your life. Choose a young, not too salty goat cheese.

3 cups cut watermelon

3 ounces new, young goat cheese

1 teaspoon thyme or lemon thyme leaves (1 large or several small twigs, de-leafed)

Freshly ground black pepper

Kosher salt

On a clean surface (melon picks up off flavors easily), cut the watermelon into slices and those, in turn, into pointed shards about as long as your finger. Put the watermelon in a bowl and add the goat cheese, breaking it up as you scatter it around. Sprinkle on the thyme leaves, a solid grind of pepper, and just a tiny pinch of salt. Toss and taste.

Triple Sage T-Bone:
Sage Butter, Fried Sage Leaves, and Scattered Fresh Sage with Roasted Tomatoes

I love sage. Its velvety blue-gray leaves conceal a nutty, astringent flavor that makes almost any meat taste better. Just smelling it is evocative—but that's because I grew up riding my horse through it out in Idaho, where sagebrush, the domestic herb's giant cousin, grows in endless wild tufts. The dot-matrix effect of these bushes gives the dry hills their deceptively lush look.

More subtle than you'd expect, this steak is easy to pair with other sides, but I like it with Roasted Tomatoes and Grilled Bread (page 119).

Serves 4
GRILL OR PAN-FRY

4 T-bone steaks

1 teaspoon kosher salt

Olive oil for rubbing

1 to 2 tablespoons peanut oil for pan-frying

SAGE BUTTER

8 sage leaves, chopped

1 large shallot, finely chopped

4 tablespoons unsalted butter, softened

Kosher salt and freshly ground black pepper

FRIED SAGE LEAVES

20 to 25 whole sage leaves

1/3 cup olive oil

Kosher salt

1 sage leaf, in strips, for garnish

Prepare your steaks by generously salting them, then allow them to come to room temperature. Rub with olive oil just before cooking.

To make the sage butter, combine the chopped sage, shallots, and butter, using a fork to mash it all together. Salt and pepper the mix generously and set aside. Do not refrigerate.

To make the fried sage leaves, remove the stems and place the sage in a large frying pan with the oil at *very* low heat. Frying the sage will take a while, 30 to 45 minutes. Don't rush it. It should almost seem as if the sage isn't cooking at all. It is slowly becoming crisp and, by the end, ever so slightly brown around the edges. There's no need to turn the leaves since they're so thin—both sides are exposed to the hot oil. When the leaves are crisp and just barely browning, carefully remove them from the pan with a spatula, salt lightly, and set aside. If you're going to pan-fry your steak, don't wash that pan! Cook your steak in the delicious, sage-infused oil in the bottom.

To grill, your coals should be so hot that you can comfortably keep your hand 2 inches above the grate for 3 seconds—just! (For gas grills, this means 450°F.) Put the oiled steaks on the hottest part of the grill and sear for 3 to 5 minutes on each side over high heat before you begin to fuss over them. That means moving the steaks to a cooler part of the grill, and cooking for another 8 to 15 minutes while flipping, poking, and watching as you work toward crispy-brown perfection. **To pan-fry,** heat a little additional peanut oil in a heavy pan with the sage-flavored olive oil until it's very hot—almost smoking. Sear the steaks for 3 minutes on each side over high heat before turning down the burner. Cook over moderate heat for an additional 8 to 15 minutes, turning the steaks every few minutes as they brown. For very thick T-bones, you might want to finish cooking them by putting them, pan and all, in a 400°F oven.

However you cook your steaks, check for doneness often, using the finger-poke method, an instant-read thermometer (120° to 130°F for rare to medium-rare), or the nick-and-peek method (see page 19). After cooking, rest the steaks for 5 minutes in a warming oven (170°F) or on a warm plate under a loose tent of foil.

Before serving, salt the steaks and give them a grind of fresh black pepper. Finish by slathering each steak with the sage butter, using it all. Distribute the fried sage leaves over the melting butter and top that with a few very fine strips of fresh sage. Give each plate a Roasted Tomato and some of that crispy Grilled Bread before bringing it to the table.

Roasted Tomatoes

First you gut the tomatoes and then stuff them with aromatics such as basil and garlic. A sprinkling of Parmigiano-Reggiano is what makes these tomatoes sing, but getting the water out is what makes them so sweet. Use good summer tomatoes and you'll be a convert.

4 tomatoes

1 tablespoon olive oil

1 clove garlic, minced

1 teaspoon raw sugar (see page 29)

1/2 teaspoon kosher salt

2 tablespoons chopped basil leaves, plus more for garnish

2 tablespoons freshly grated Parmigiano-Reggiano, plus more for garnish

Kosher salt and freshly ground black pepper

Preheat the oven to 400°F. Prepare the tomatoes by coring them and then using your finger to clear the flesh and juice from the center (reserve the juice). You want the tomato partly hollowed out with a hole on top. Work gently and if you squeeze a little as you try to get some of the juice out, try not to split the tomato (I usually do—you can still use it). Place the reserved liquid, tomato pulp, and any solids in a small saucepan. Add the olive oil, garlic, sugar, and salt and cook over medium heat to reduce. Remove from the heat when it has reduced by two-thirds, 5 to 8 minutes. The sauce should be thick, but the garlic should not have had a chance to brown. Stir in the basil and the Parmigiano-Reggiano, and spoon the mixture back into the hollowed-out tomatoes.

Bake in a shallow dish, uncovered, for 20 to 30 minutes, depending on the size of the tomatoes. When you take them out of the oven, they should be starting to brown but still holding their shape.

Before serving, sprinkle on a pinch of kosher salt and a few grinds of black pepper. Finish with a fine grating of Parmigiano-Reggiano and some chopped basil.

Strip Steak

with Fresh Horseradish-Watercress Sauce, Potato Salad, and Irish Peas

Vivid green on the plate, the watercress and its peppery, grassy taste dominate this sauce, with the horseradish adding bite. Paired with Potato Salad and Irish Peas, this makes a brilliant meal. The potato salad isn't heavy at all—I've used my version of the versatile Greek sauce, tzatziki, as a dressing. Of course, the peas are out of this world when made with fresh shell peas, picked right from the garden—or lugged home that day from the farmers' market.

Serves 4

GRILL OR PAN-FRY

4 strip steaks

1 teaspoon kosher salt

Olive oil for rubbing

1 to 2 tablespoons peanut oil for pan-frying

FRESH HORSERADISH-WATERCRESS SAUCE

4- to 5-inch piece fresh horseradish

1 tablespoon white wine vinegar

1 bunch watercress

1/4 teaspoon raw sugar (see page 29)

1/2 teaspoon kosher salt

1 cup whole-fat Greek yogurt (I like Fage), crème fraîche, or sour cream

Prepare the steaks by salting them and letting them come to room temperature. Rub with olive oil just before cooking.

To make the sauce, peel the horseradish and grate as finely as possible. I use a food processor for the job. It's possible to use a Microplane or a box grater, but it's heavy work to shred this woody root. Once grated, measure out 3/4 cup, then add the vinegar and mix. Set aside for at least 30 minutes. This is called macerating; it's a way of breaking down the rough fibers.

No need to pick through all the watercress, piece by piece. Just hold it as you would hold a bouquet and chop off the bottom third of the stems (you should have about 2 cups stemmed). Return the horseradish and vinegar mix to the food processor (use a blender if you don't have a food processor). Add the watercress, sugar, and salt and let the machine do its work. Once you've worked it thoroughly (3 minutes at minimum), add the yogurt and pulse again until smooth.

Taste. The sauce should be smooth, without little rough shreds, and it should have a nice bite without being unpleasantly spicy. (You can correct for this by adding more yogurt.)

To grill, your coals should be so hot that you can comfortably keep your hand 2 inches above the grate for 3 seconds—just! (For gas grills, this means 450°F.) Put the oiled steaks on the hottest part of the grill and sear for 3 minutes on each side over intense heat before you begin to fuss over them. That means moving the steaks to a cooler part of the grill and cooking more gently for an additional 6 to 10 minutes, flipping, poking, and watching as you work toward crispy-brown perfection.

To pan-fry, heat the peanut oil in a heavy pan until it's very hot—almost smoking. Sear the steaks for 3 minutes on each side over high heat before turning down the burner. Cook the steaks over moderate heat for an additional 6 to 10 minutes, turning the steaks every few minutes as they slowly brown. If your steaks are more than 2 inches thick, you may want to finish cooking them by putting them, pan and all, in a 400°F oven.

However you cook your steaks, check for doneness often, using the finger-poke method, an instant-read thermometer (120° to 130°F for rare to medium-rare), or the nick-and-peek method (see page 19). After cooking, rest the steaks for 5 minutes in a warming oven (170°F) or on a warm plate under a loose tent of foil.

To serve, I like to pool the sauce under the meat, which looks pretty on a white plate, but you can serve the sauce on the side if you'd rather. The Potato Salad and Irish Peas round out the plate.

Potato Salad

I like to use a combination of yellow, red, and purple potatoes to make this salad; they look great mixed with the yogurt and herbs.

$1/2$ seedless European cucumber, skin on

$1^1/2$ teaspoons kosher salt

2 pounds potatoes (Yellow Finn and red-skinned potatoes are best; if you're mixing, add a few Purple Peruvian potatoes for color)

$3/4$ cup Greek yogurt (Total or 2% Fage is terrific)

1 to 2 shallots, chopped (3 tablespoons)

2 tablespoons lemon juice

2 tablespoons chopped dill

1 tablespoon chopped mint

1 clove garlic, minced

Freshly ground black pepper

Dill, chopped, for garnish

Mint sprig, chopped, for garnish

Pinch of Maldon salt

Cut the cucumber into thin slices. Stack a manageable pile of the slices on the counter and cut across them 3 times, creating chunky matchsticks. Repeat. Put the cut cucumber in a bowl with 1 teaspoon of the salt and toss. Set aside for 30 minutes.

Bring a large pot of water to a boil and add the potatoes. If the potatoes aren't the same size, cut them for even cooking. Cook for 15 to 25 minutes, depending on the size of the potatoes. Check for doneness with a fork. The center of the largest potato should be firm but not hard. When the potatoes are tender, drain them, rinse briefly with cold water, and allow them to cool before cutting into slices. Put the slices in a large mixing bowl and set aside.

In a small bowl, combine the yogurt, shallot, lemon juice, dill, mint, and garlic. Beat the dressing with the remaining $1/2$ teaspoon of salt and some freshly ground black pepper and set aside.

Drain any water from the cucumbers and put them on a clean dish towel. Squeeze the towel to remove as much water as possible. Don't worry about crushing the pieces. Put the slices in the bowl with the potatoes and add the dressing. Toss gently until the potatoes are just coated, and taste for salt. Sprinkle on a little chopped dill and mint along with a final grind of black pepper and a pinch of Maldon salt before serving.

Irish Peas

If you don't have fresh peas, this recipe can be made with those frosty green pellets from the frozen food aisle at the grocery store. The mint and butter make even those peas tasty.

2 cups fresh English shell peas (or whatever you can get)

1 tablespoon butter

1 tablespoon chopped fresh mint

Kosher salt and freshly ground black pepper

Bring a pot of salted water to a boil. When the water is roiling, pour the peas in and allow them to cook for just 1 minute before draining (frozen peas will need three times as long). After draining the peas, return them to the empty pot and add the butter, mint, and a pinch of salt and black pepper. Toss and serve.

Risotto and Strip Steak
Scattered with Olives, Parsley, Pine Nuts, Lemon Peel, and Parmesan

What makes this recipe work is the earthy combination of olives and Parmesan; the parsley and lemon add freshness, the pine nuts richness and texture. The first time I made it, I was dreaming of Italian flavors while relying on the ingredients I'd normally put in what my family calls "Pasta Nada"—that is, what you put on pasta when there's nothing left in the refrigerator but a stray lemon, pine nuts, and a big hunk of Parmesan. I love steak this way, and it goes great with any red wine. The risotto is crucial and benefits greatly from the treatment. Grilled Bread (page 119) would be a fine thing to have with this meal, too.

Serves 4

GRILL OR PAN-FRY

4 strip steaks

1 teaspoon kosher salt

1 clove garlic, peeled and cut in half

Olive oil for rubbing

1/4 cup pine nuts, toasted and salted

1/2 teaspoon whole fennel seeds, toasted and ground

1 to 2 tablespoons peanut oil for pan-frying

2 tablespoons chopped parsley

1 tablespoon chopped oregano

1 lemon, zested

1/3 cup Niçoise, kalamata, or dry-cured olives, pitted and coarsely chopped

1/3 cup grated Parmigiano-Reggiano

Freshly ground black pepper and kosher salt

1 tablespoon your best olive oil

Prepare your steak by salting it and then rubbing the garlic halves over it. Allow the steaks to come to room temperature, and rub with olive oil just before cooking.

Before cooking the steak, get your supporting ingredients ready and set them aside until your steak is ready to be served. To toast the nuts and fennel seeds, a cast-iron pan works best. They should be fragrant and ever so slightly browned.

To grill, your coals should be so hot that you can comfortably keep your hand 2 inches above the grate for 3 seconds—just! (For gas grills, this means 450°F.) Put the oiled steak on the hottest part of the grill and sear for 3 to 5 minutes over intense heat on each side before you begin to fuss over it. That means moving the steak to a cooler part of the grill and finishing over more gentle heat for 6 to 10 minutes while flipping, poking, and watching as you work them toward crispy-brown perfection. **To pan-fry,** heat the peanut oil in a heavy pan until it's very hot—almost smoking. Sear the steak for 3 minutes on each side over high heat before turning down the burner. Cook over moderate heat for an additional 6 to 10 minutes, turning the steaks every few minutes as they slowly brown. If your kitchen is filling with smoke, finish cooking the steak by putting it, pan and all, in a 400°F oven.

However you cook your steak, check for doneness often, using the finger-poke method, an instant-read thermometer (120° to 130°F for rare to medium-rare), or the nick-and-peek method (see page 19). After cooking, rest the steaks for 5 minutes in a warming oven (170°F) or on a warm plate under a loose tent of foil.

Serve the steaks on warm plates along with a scoop of risotto, then scatter the parsley, oregano, fennel seeds, pine nuts, lemon zest, olives, and cheese over everything. Give the whole thing a good dose of freshly ground black pepper and a sprinkle of kosher salt before drizzling on some of your very best olive oil. Finish with a quick squeeze of lemon—go easy—and you're done.

Risotto

Raw ingredients, as with any other simple food, matter here. Use the best, fresh Parmigiano-Reggiano, high-end olive oil, rich stock, and Italian Arborio rice with a date. No need to boil your stock or fuss over adding tiny quantities at a time.

Double the recipe if you want great leftovers

1 cup Italian Arborio rice

2 tablespoons unsalted butter

2 tablespoons chicken juices (see page 22)

$1/2$ teaspoon kosher salt

$2^1/2$ to 3 cups chicken stock (page 26), at room temperature

$1/2$ lemon, zest only

1 tablespoon freshly grated Parmigiano-Reggiano, plus more for garnish

2 tablespoons your best olive oil

Freshly ground black pepper (optional)

In a heavy pot, combine the rice and butter. Cook over medium heat, stirring constantly, for 2 to 3 minutes. You want to coat the rice and let it absorb some of the butter while it gets a little toasty. Add the chicken juices and salt and stir. Once it's hot, add 1 cup of the chicken stock. Stir some more, scraping the bottom of the pot as you go.

Reduce your heat to low and allow the risotto to absorb the stock. No need to stand and stir. Just keep an eye on it and add another $1/2$ cup of stock when it starts to stick and most of the liquid has been absorbed. Keep adding stock until the rice has absorbed 2 cups of stock total.

At this point, take a taste and feel the grain of the rice. It's almost certainly still too chewy, but try to get a sense of the rice's texture. You'll need to add stock more slowly now to avoid overcooking the rice. Your goal is rice that still has some of its structure left but with a pleasant give—chewy but not crunchy. As with anything, the rice will continue to cook after you take it off the heat. When you've added the last bit of stock, grate in a little lemon zest. Add the cheese and finish with the olive oil. Before serving, taste for salt and add some freshly ground black pepper if you want to. Once it's on the plate, a finishing grate of cheese is delicious and pretty.

T-Bone with Fava Beans,
Purple Potatoes, Ramps, and Crispy Slab Bacon

Fava beans are a pain. First you have to shuck them, then blanch the beans so that you can pop each little gem out of the shell. But you know what? They're worth it. And they're only around for a few fleeting weeks in spring. This steak takes advantage of that moment—combining favas, ramps, and purple potatoes, for a spring meal. The bacon just pushes everything up a notch.

Serves 4

GRILL OR PAN-FRY

4 T-bone steaks

1 teaspoon kosher salt

Olive oil for rubbing

2 pounds fava beans, in the pod

12 spring ramps, with bulbs about the size of a thumb, or spring onions, green garlic, or leeks

1/4 pound slab bacon, cut into small cubes, or the best, thick-cut bacon you can find

Kosher salt and freshly ground black pepper

1 teaspoon minced fresh rosemary

Prepare your steaks by salting them, then let them come to room temperature. Rub with a bit of olive oil just before cooking.

Before you shell the favas, bring a pot of water to a boil. Once the beans are shelled, pop them in the boiling water. Allow the water to return to a boil, and then remove from the heat and shock the beans by draining and dousing them with icy water. Next, remove the tough outer shell either by pinching or peeling each bean; you'll find your method. Place the beans in a bowl and set aside. You should have about 1 cup.

Trim the ramps by cutting off the fringed roots and the top 2 to 3 inches of their distinctive green leaves. Holding them as a bunch, slice the leafy tops across, starting from the top and working down. Stop cutting when you reach the transition between the purple-green and the white bulb. Leave the remaining bulb and white stem whole unless they are large. Golf ball–size bulbs and anything bigger should be cut in half lengthwise. Set the cut leaves and bulbs aside.

Cook the cubes of bacon slowly, over gentle heat, until crisp. Place them on a towel and drain all the grease that will easily pour out; reserve the grease. Cook the favas and ramps together in the same pan using the remaining bacon grease. Do it fast and hot, adding salt to taste. Really, you want the flavors to be strong and fresh, so just cook to soften and heat, 5 minutes at most. Salt and set aside in a warm oven.

To grill, your coals should be so hot that you can comfortably keep your hand 2 inches above the grate for 3 seconds—just! (For gas grills, this means 450°F.) Put the oiled steaks on the hottest part of the grill and sear for 3 to 5 minutes on each side over high heat before you begin to fuss over them. That means moving the steaks to a cooler part of the grill to cook for an additional 8 to 15 minutes over more moderate heat, flipping, poking, and watching as you work toward crispy-brown perfection. **To pan-fry,** heat the bacon pan until it is very hot. If necessary, use two pans, adding a little of the reserved grease to the second pan. Sear the steaks for 3 minutes on each side over high heat before turning down the burner. Cook over moderate heat for an additional 8 to 15 minutes, turning the steaks every few minutes as they slowly brown. If smoke is a problem, put the steaks, pan and all, in a 400°F oven to finish cooking.

However you cook your steaks, check for doneness often, using the finger-poke method, an instant-read thermometer (120° to 130°F for rare to medium-rare), or the nick-and-peek method (see page 19). Salt the steaks and then rest them for 5 minutes in a warming oven (170°F) or on a warm plate under a loose tent of foil.

To serve, center each steak on a warm plate and arrange some of the potatoes around it. Next, scatter the ramps and fava beans over it and around it on the plate itself. Do the same with the bacon, giving everything a grind of black pepper and a sprinkle of rosemary before serving.

Purple Potatoes

1 pound purple potatoes, skin on (Purple Peruvian are good)

1 teaspoon kosher salt

1 tablespoon white vinegar

1 tablespoon your best olive oil

To cook the potatoes, boil a pot of water with the salt. Add the potatoes and the vinegar, which helps bind the color. Cook until tender. How long this takes depends, of course, on the size of your potatoes. Purple potatoes can range from the size of a large wine grape to the more spudlike proportions of a giant Idaho baker, so use a fork to test after 15 minutes. When the potatoes are cooked through but not mushy, remove them from the heat, drain them, and keep them warm until everything else is ready. Slice the potatoes into 1/2-inch rounds to show off the purple center flesh and the contrasting dark skin. Gently toss with the olive oil.

Warwick-Style Coffee-Rubbed Filet
with Vanilla Sauce, Jasmine Rice, and Hazelnut Green Beans

Okay. I know this sounds unusual. But it's delicious, delicate, and complex all at the same time. A couple of years ago I ate a version of this at the house of a friend—he also happens to be a great and adventurous cook—and it really stuck with me. That was in Warwick, New York. Banish the association between sweetness and vanilla and you'll be well on your way to the pleasures of combining a subtly spiced steak with a rich sauce, the incredible scent of jasmine rice (page 165), and the beauty of Hazelnut Green Beans.

Serves 4

GRILL OR PAN-FRY

4 filets (or use hangar, skirt, or a top loin steak)

Olive oil for rubbing

2 tablespoons peanut oil for pan-frying

COFFEE RUB

1 teaspoon whole black peppercorns

1 teaspoon whole coriander

2 juniper berries

1 teaspoon kosher salt

1 tablespoon raw sesame seeds

1/4 teaspoon ground cloves

1/2 teaspoon cinnamon

1/2 teaspoon raw sugar (see page 29)

1 teaspoon freshly ground coffee

To make the rub, use a mortar and pestle to thoroughly grind the peppercorns, coriander, juniper berries, and salt. Add the sesame seeds, cloves, cinnamon, sugar, and coffee. Mix it all together and sprinkle it on the steaks. Use it all, patting the rub on so it adheres to the steak. Let them come to room temperature. Rub the steak gently with olive oil before cooking.

To make the sauce, in a sauté pan, combine the butter and shallots. Cook gently for 1 to 2 minutes, until just soft. Add the vinegar, chicken juices, and vanilla bean. Stir and bring the sauce back to a simmer before adding the cream. (If you're using stock rather than chicken juices, cook the sauce for 3 to 6 minutes, until reduced by half, before adding the cream.) Allow the sauce to reduce slightly, simmering over gentle heat. Once it has thickened slightly, fish out the vanilla bean and, using the edge of a butter knife, scrape out the pulpy center. Return the bean and pulp to the sauce.

The sugar in the rub means that these steaks will brown quickly—they may even blacken a little. **To grill,** your coals should be so hot that you can comfortably keep your hand 2 inches above the grate for 3 seconds—just! (For gas grills, this means 450°F.) Put the oiled steaks on the hottest part of the grill and sear for 3 to 5 minutes on each side over high heat before you begin to fuss over them. That means moving the steaks to a cooler part of the grill and cooking for an additional 6 to 10 minutes over more moderate heat, flipping, poking, and watching as you work toward crispy-brown perfection. Filet is lean and delicate. Serve it rare. **To pan-fry,** heat the peanut oil in a heavy pan until it's very hot—almost smoking. Sear the steaks for 3 minutes on each side over high heat before turning down the burner. Cook over moderate heat for an additional 6 to 10 minutes, turning the steaks every few

VANILLA SAUCE

2 tablespoons unsalted butter

1 shallot, chopped (about
2 tablespoons)

1 tablespoon champagne
vinegar

3 tablespoons chicken juices
(see page 22) or $^{1}/_{2}$ cup chicken
stock (page 26)

1 vanilla bean, split lengthwise,
or $^{1}/_{2}$ teaspoon vanilla paste

1 cup cream or half-and-half

$^{1}/_{2}$ teaspoon kosher salt

minutes as they slowly brown. If smoke is a problem, put the steaks, pan and all, in a 400°F oven to finish cooking.

However you cook your steaks, check for doneness often, using the finger-poke method, an instant-read thermometer (120° to 130°F for rare to medium-rare), or the nick-and-peek method (see page 19). After cooking, give the meat a pinch of salt and let it rest for 5 minutes in a warming oven (170°F) or on a warm plate under a loose tent of foil.

To serve, spoon the sauce onto 4 warm plates and place the steaks on top. Add some jasmine rice and Hazelnut Green Beans to finish.

Hazelnut Green Beans

Buy good French hazelnut oil with a date printed on the can, as it is highly perishable. Store in the refrigerator and use it often on salads and vegetables.

3 cups green beans, trimmed

1 tablespoon kosher salt

1 tablespoon olive oil or
unsalted butter

1 tablespoon hazelnut oil or your
best olive oil

$^{1}/_{4}$ cup hazelnuts, toasted and
finely chopped

Freshly ground black pepper

Cook the green beans in a pot of boiling water with the salt for 5 to 8 minutes, depending on how big and how fresh they are. Test one; it should be tender but still a little crunchy. Remove from the heat and shock the beans by dumping them into icy cold water. Drain and set aside to dry until you're 5 minutes from eating.

When your steaks are almost done, put the olive oil into a large frying pan, add the beans, and toss until heated through. Keep the heat fairly low. You want the beans quite hot, but you don't want to scorch the oil or overcook them. When they're done, transfer to a warm serving bowl, drizzle with the hazelnut oil, and toss with the nuts. Grind on some black pepper and taste for seasoning. Add salt as needed.

Rib Steak with Bing Cherry–Pinot Noir Reduction,

Cauliflower Mash, and Glazed Carrots

The sauce is rich, with the cherries adding a little sweetness but mostly a tart contrast that wakes up the lusty rib steak. I'd run just about anything around in this sauce, but Cauliflower Mash and Glazed Carrots are perfect with it. The Cauliflower Mash is rich but lighter than potatoes, with a distinctly cruciferous flavor, while the Glazed Carrots are earthy and sweet.

Serves 4

GRILL OR PAN-FRY

4 rib steaks, bone-in or boneless

1 teaspoon kosher salt

Olive oil for rubbing

1 to 2 tablespoons peanut oil for pan-frying

BING CHERRY–PINOT NOIR REDUCTION

2 shallots, minced

3 tablespoons unsalted butter

2 cups pinot noir, or Shiraz or Merlot

2 dozen fresh Bing cherries, pitted

3 tablespoons chicken juices (see page 22) or $1/2$ cup chicken stock (page 26)

Prepare the steaks by salting them, and then let them come to room temperature. Rub with a bit of olive oil just before cooking.

To make the sauce, quickly sauté the shallots in 2 tablespoons of the butter to soften, about 2 minutes. Add the wine, cherries, and chicken juices before the butter browns. Cook the sauce 10 to 15 minutes, to reduce to about $1/2$ cup, stirring frequently. When it's done, the sauce should be thick and rich—the consistency of heated jam. If you're working with chicken stock, not chicken juices, reduce the sauce a little longer—as long as 20 minutes. Set the sauce aside until the steaks are resting.

To grill, your coals should be so hot that you can comfortably keep your hand 2 inches above the grate for 3 seconds—just! (For gas grills, this means 450°F.) Put the oiled steaks on the hottest part of the grill and sear for 3 to 5 minutes on each side over high heat before you begin to fuss over them. That means moving the steaks to a cooler part of the grill and cooking for an additional 8 to 12 minutes over moderate heat, flipping, poking, and watching as you work toward crispy-brown perfection. **To pan-fry,** heat the peanut oil in a heavy pan until it's very hot—almost smoking. Sear the steaks for 3 minutes on each side over high heat before turning down the burner. Cook over moderate heat for an additional 8 to 12 minutes, turning the steaks every few minutes as they slowly brown. If your steaks are more than 2 inches thick, you may want to finish cooking them by putting them, pan and all, in a 400°F oven.

However you cook your steaks, check for doneness often, using the finger-poke method, an instant-read thermometer (120° to 130°F for rare to medium-rare), or the nick-and-peek method (see page 19). After cooking, rest the steaks for 5 minutes in a warming oven (170°F) or on a warm plate under a loose tent of foil.

While the steaks are resting, finish the sauce by gently reheating and adding that final 1 tablespoon of butter. Next, get your plates ready with the steak, a neat scoop of Cauliflower Mash for each, and some of the bright, glossy carrots. The sauce should go over the steak last. It will happily find its way around the plate.

Cauliflower Mash

The Cinderella-like transformation that takes place here relies almost entirely on a food processor—you'll definitely need one.

1 head cauliflower (about 2 pounds)

2 tablespoons unsalted butter

1 teaspoon kosher salt

Chop off the stem of the cauliflower and break up the remainder into florets. Put the cauliflower in a steam basket over water in a pot with a lid. Make sure you have water up to the basket. Bring it to a boil, and cook for 10 to 12 minutes, or until the cauliflower is tender. Drain and coarsely mash the florets with a potato masher before transfering the cooked cauliflower to a food processor. Add the butter and salt and blend until smoothe, 1 to 2 minutes. Scrape the mash into a bowl and it's ready to serve.

Glazed Carrots

Buy carrots with the tops still on—they're fresher and taste a whole lot better than the packaged varieties.

1 teaspoon sugar (raw if you have it; see page 29)

1 teaspoon kosher salt

2 tablespoons unsalted butter or olive oil

2 tablespoons water

6 good-size carrots, peeled and cut in half lengthwise and then in half again

Put all the ingredients in a heavy pot and cover. Cook, over very low heat, until the carrots are tender. Shake the pot frequently so the carrots don't stick and burn. They should be done in less than 10 minutes. You'll know when they're soft and the pan has gotten dangerously dry. Catch them just before this happens; a dry pot will enable the sugar to truly caramelize, but if you wait too long they will blacken. Transfer to a warm bowl.

Hangar Steak
with French Feta, Salsa Verde, and Mint-Zucchini Pancakes

This is a delicious dish inspired by Suzanne Goin's recipe for lamb in her terrific book *Sunday Suppers at Lucques.* I've added some chives here and made the salsa more minty than parsley-flavored. I've always been a French feta fan; I use it all too predictably in my salads. But I had never combined its briny, sheepy essence with red meat, as Suzanne does. The Mint-Zucchini Pancakes take to feta and salsa verde as effortlessly as the hangar steak does.

Serves 4
GRILL OR PAN-FRY

2 pounds hangar steak

1 teaspoon kosher salt

Olive oil for rubbing

1 to 2 tablespoons peanut oil for pan-frying

SALSA VERDE

1/4 cup fresh oregano leaves, chopped

1/4 cup parsley leaves, chopped

1/2 cup mint leaves, chopped

4 long stalks chives, chopped

1 clove garlic, peeled and crushed

2 anchovy filets, chopped

5 capers

1/2 teaspoon kosher salt

Freshly ground black pepper

1 tablespoon lemon juice

1/3 cup good olive oil

4 ounces French feta (my favorite is Valbreso)

If you buy a whole hangar steak, you'll need to remove the tendon that runs down its center. It's best to do this with a freshly sharpened filet knife to avoid damaging the meat. Because the tendon runs down the center of the steak, you'll be cutting first on one side and then on the other, creating two long pieces of meat that look like irregular, short filets. Beginning at the thickest end of the steak and working down its length, cut along one side of the tendon, keeping your knife as close to the white tendon as possible.

Salt the steak and let it come to room temperature, then rub with a bit of olive oil just before cooking.

To make the salsa, put the oregano, parsley, mint, chives, garlic, anchovy, and capers into a large mortar (or use a food processor). Add the salt and some freshly ground pepper. Grind to a fine paste. Stir in the lemon juice and olive oil. Taste. It should have a little bite of acidity from the lemon, but no single flavor should dominate. The anchovy and feta are salty, so don't add additional salt now.

To grill, your coals should be so hot that you can comfortably keep your hand 2 inches above the grate for 3 seconds— just! (For gas grills, this means 450°F.) Put the oiled steak on the hottest part of the grill and sear for 3 to 5 minutes on each side before you begin to fuss over it. That means moving the steak to a cooler part of the grill and cooking for an additional 10 to 14 minutes over moderate heat, flipping, poking, and watching as you work toward crispy-brown perfection. **To pan-fry,** heat the peanut oil in a heavy pan until it's very hot—almost smoking. Sear the steak for 3 minutes on each side over high heat before turning down the burner. Cook over moderate heat for an additional 10 to 14 minutes, turning the steak every few minutes as it slowly browns.

Hangar steak can be uneven—thick in one spot, thinner in another. Strike a balance and check for doneness often, using the finger-poke method, an instant-read thermometer (120° to 130°F for rare to medium-rare), or the nick-and-peek method (see page 19). Once the steak is cooked, rest it in a warming oven (170°F) or on a warm plate under a loose tent of foil for 5 minutes.

To serve, slice the steak across, creating nice thick rounds that look almost like minifilets. Tuck them together on the plate, give the meat a pinch of salt, and put a Mint-Zucchini Pancake opposite. Finally, spoon a generous portion of the Salsa Verde over the steak. Scatter the feta over everything and serve.

Mint-Zucchini Pancakes

Zucchini are the essence of late summer; they bully everything else in the garden with their tireless growth. I like to dispense with these monsters in ways that don't involve a steamer basket or the word *bread*. If you're using a giant zucchini, be sure to peel and seed it.

4 cups grated zucchini (3 small zucchinis or 1 late-August monster)

1 leek, white end and a little of the tender light green part

1 tablespoon kosher salt

2 eggs

1/2 cup milk

1/2 cup matzo meal or fine breadcrumbs

1/4 cup fresh mint leaves, chopped

Freshly ground black pepper

1 to 2 tablespoons olive oil, plus more as needed

1 tablespoon unsalted butter, plus more as needed

Shred the zucchini using a food processor or a box grater. Chop the leek and combine it with the zucchini and salt in a mixing bowl. Let the mixture sit for at least 20 minutes (and up to an hour) to allow the salt to extract the water from the vegetables. When you're ready to cook the pancakes, drain the excess water from the bowl and dump the zucchini-leek mixture into a clean dish towel. Wrap into a ball and wring, squeezing to get as much of the water out as possible.

Return the squeezed ball of zucchini to your bowl and add the eggs, milk, matzo meal, mint, and black pepper. Mix well. Heat a heavy frying pan over medium-high heat with 1 tablespoon of the oil and the butter. When it's hot (test with a shred of zucchini batter—if it sizzles madly, go), use a soup-spoon to drop in a saucer-size round of the batter. Turn the heat down a bit, flatten, and cook. You want crunchy, quick-cooking pancakes that don't absorb a lot of oil, but you don't want to burn them either. Add more oil and butter as needed.

After browning both sides, sprinkle with kosher salt and transfer the pancakes to a paper towel–lined plate in a warm oven until ready to serve.

Cowboy Steak
Juniper Berry Rub, Caramelized Onions, and Pan-Fried Sweet Potatoes

I love juniper berries. When I was a kid, I used to pick them in the woods up the creek from our house in Aspen. My mom threatened to make gin. I did nothing more with them than mix them with water in a glass jar to create a fragrant fairy brew. But I don't doubt flavor-starved cowboys—or maybe hungry prospectors—used these pungent little berries to spice up their bland food. With the sweetness of the onions and potatoes, this is grown-up camp food.

Serves 4

GRILL OR PAN-FRY

10 dried juniper berries

1 teaspoon kosher salt

4 bone-in strip steaks (cowboy steak!)

Olive oil for rubbing

1 to 2 tablespoons peanut oil for pan-frying

Freshly ground black pepper

Grind up the juniper berries with the salt using your mortar and pestle or a spice grinder and coat the steak with the mixture. Allow the meat to come to room temperature. Rub with a bit of olive oil just before cooking.

To grill, your coals should be so hot that you can comfortably keep your hand 2 inches above the grate for 3 seconds—just! (For gas grills, this means 450°F.) Put the oiled steaks on the hottest part of the grill and sear for 3 to 5 minutes on each side over high heat before you begin to fuss over them. That means moving the steaks to a cooler part of the grill and cooking for an additional 8 to 12 minutes over moderate heat, flipping, poking, and watching as you work toward crispy-brown perfection. **To pan-fry,** heat the peanut oil in a heavy pan until it's very hot—almost smoking. Sear the steaks for 3 minutes on each side over high heat before turning down the burner. Cook over moderate heat for an additional 8 to 12 minutes, turning the steaks every few minutes as they slowly brown. If you've bought big fat steaks (more than 2 inches thick), you might want to finish cooking them by putting them, pan and all, in a 400°F oven.

However you cook your steaks, check for doneness often, using the finger-poke method, an instant-read thermometer (120° to 130°F for rare to medium-rare), or the nick-and-peek method (see page 19). Bone-in steaks do take a little longer to cook. After cooking, rest the steaks in a warming oven (170°F) or on a warm plate under a loose tent of foil for 5 minutes.

To serve, give each steak a final sprinkle of salt and a grind of fresh black pepper as you place it in the center of a warm plate. Pile some Caramelized Onions on top of each steak and surround with Pan-Fried Sweet Potatoes.

Caramelized Onions

2 tablespoons unsalted butter

2 yellow or red onions, peeled and thinly sliced (I like to use Vidalia)

In a heavy pan over very low heat (really!), heat the butter, add the onions, and wait, stirring occasionally. It takes some time for the sugars to come out and then to slowly brown, so don't rush it. The onions should be a nice, mellow brown after 20 minutes or so. If you need the pan, transfer the onions to a warming oven until you're ready to pile them on the steak.

Pan-Fried Sweet Potatoes

Inspired by a recipe in Edna Lewis's lovely book *The Taste of the Country*, these yams are fast and easy to make. Think fresh yam taste, crispy edges, and soft centers.

2 large yams, the longer the better, skin on

1 tablespoon unsalted butter

1 tablespoon olive oil

Kosher salt and freshly ground pepper

Slice the yams into $1/4$-inch slices. Heat the butter and oil together in two large, heavy frying pans, or work in batches. Lay the slices in the pan, flipping to coat with the hot oil on both sides. Once they're coated, cook gently on each side for 8 to 10 minutes, or until golden brown. You want the center soft and the edges so they're just beginning to curl as they crisp. Drain on a rack or on paper towels, salt and pepper generously, and set in a warming oven until needed.

Monterey Cheesesteak
with Beet Chips and Kohlrabi Salad

This cheesesteak, like the Philadelphia version, follows the guiding principle of all serious guy-cooking: any food worth eating is better with melted cheese. (Think nachos, cheeseburgers, chili, and cheese dogs.) Use the best plain Cheddar you can get or try a good pepper cheese. On the East Coast, I like Cabot's Habanero Cheddar, which is easy to find and melts nicely. As a side, freshly made Beet Chips are pretty special. They're sweeter than potato chips and easy to get perfectly crunchy. I make them when the weather has turned cool, using baseball-size fall beets. The Kohlrabi Salad provides a dose of raw vegetables made delicious by feta, olive oil, and cracker bread.

Serves 4

PAN-FRY, THEN BROIL

1 large porterhouse (about 2 pounds)

1 1/2 teaspoons red pepper flakes

1 teaspoon kosher salt

Olive oil for rubbing

1 to 2 tablespoons peanut oil for pan-frying

Cheddar with hot peppers, 6 to 8 thinly sliced pieces, or enough to cover the steak's surface

Coat the steaks with the red pepper flakes and salt. Distribute the pepper flakes with your hand, rubbing them over the meat so they stick. Allow the steak to come to room temperature and rub with a bit of olive oil just before cooking.

Preheat the oven to 400°F. Heat the peanut oil in a cast-iron pan until it's nearly smoking, then put the steak in the pan. Sear for about 3 minutes on each side, until crispy and brown. Move the steak from the stovetop to the oven, using the same pan. For very thick steak (2 inches and up), broil for 2 to 3 minutes before putting the thinly sliced cheese on top; for thinner steak, put the cheese on before you put the steak in the oven, then broil for 3 to 5 minutes total. When you take the steak out, you want the cheese gently melted and the steak rare to medium-rare, 120° to 130°F at the center. Rest the steak on a warm plate under a loose tent of foil for 5 minutes.

Cut the steak into 1/2-inch-long slices. You'll see the cheese adheres nicely and you end up with pretty slices—pink in the middle with the white line of the cheese on top. Divide the slices on 4 plates and then pile on a bunch of the Beet Chips, working them up vertically into a graceful stack. Distribute the Kohlrabi Salad among the plates.

Beet Chips

3 large beets, unpeeled

3 quarts peanut or vegetable oil

Kosher salt

Trim the tops from the beets, also cutting away any of the rough, dark-colored skin around the top. Cut the beets into slices using a mandoline set to cut $1/8$-inch slices. (You could also use a knife to cut $1/8$-inch slices.) Transfer the beets to a bowl of cold water and separate them; they tend to stick together.

Heat the oil to 375°F either in a deep fryer or in a large pot on the stove. Working in batches, drop the slices into the hot oil. Avoid overcrowding. Fry the beets for 3 to 4 minutes. You want to remove them from the oil and transfer to paper towels just before they begin to visibly brown. This can be tricky with beets because you can't really see whether they are coloring. Test one for doneness at 3 minutes and judge for yourself. The chips should be very crispy but without a hint of burnt flavor. Immediately after setting the beets to drain on the towels, salt them generously.

Kohlrabi Salad

2 large kohlrabi bulbs, peeled and diced

$1/4$ cup chopped fresh mint

1 cup cherry tomatoes, cut in half

6 radishes, thinly sliced

3 ounces French feta, young goat cheese, or ricotta salata

1 cup arugula or watercress

5 pieces seeded cracker bread (I like kosher New York Sesame Flatbread)

2 tablespoons olive oil

1 tablespoon lemon juice or sherry vinegar

1 teaspoon kosher salt

Freshly ground black pepper

Combine the kohlrabi, mint, tomatoes, radishes, cheese, and arugula in a large salad bowl. Break the cracker bread into pieces and add it to the bowl. Toss, then add the oil, lemon juice, salt, and pepper. Toss again and taste. The dressing shouldn't be heavy—just a hint of lemon and olive oil.

Porterhouse
with Lemon-Artichoke Tapenade, Wild Rice, and Leafy Greens

The truth is, this tapenade is one of my favorite things to eat—on crackers, on eggs, and, of course, on steak. Wild Rice and Leafy Greens back it up nicely.

Serves 4

GRILL OR PAN-FRY

1 large porterhouse (about 2 pounds)

1 teaspoon kosher salt

Olive oil for rubbing

1 to 2 tablespoons peanut oil for pan-frying

Freshly ground black pepper

LEMON-ARTICHOKE TAPENADE

3 artichoke hearts, steamed and chopped (canned or jarred work, too; buy unadulterated hearts, without any flavoring and *not* in vinegar)

Juice of 1 lemon

Zest of 1/2 lemon

2 tablespoons olive oil

1/2 teaspoon kosher salt

Freshly ground black pepper

1 clove garlic, minced

Prepare the steak by salting it and allowing it to come to room temperature. Rub with olive oil just before cooking.

To make the tapenade, combine all the ingredients in a large mortar or in a food processor. The idea is to thoroughly blend the ingredients but not to turn them into mush. Go easy if you're using a food processor—one or two quick pulses should do the job. You should still be able to see (and taste) the individual pieces of artichoke.

To grill, your coals should be so hot that you can comfortably hold your hand 2 inches above the grate for 3 seconds—just! (For gas grills, this means 450°F.) Put the oiled steak on the hottest part of the grill and sear for 3 to 5 minutes on each side over high heat before you begin to fuss over it. That means moving the steak to a cooler part of the grill and cooking for an additional 8 to 12 minutes over moderate heat, flipping, poking, and watching as you work toward crispy-brown perfection. **To pan-fry,** heat the peanut oil in a heavy pan until it's very hot—almost smoking. Sear the steak for 3 minutes on each side over high heat before turning down the burner. Cook over moderate heat for an additional 8 to 12 minutes, turning the steak every few minutes as it slowly browns. If your house is filling with smoke, you can finish cooking the steak by putting it, pan and all, in a 400°F oven.

However you cook your steak, check for doneness often, using the finger-poke method, an instant-read thermometer (120° to 130°F for rare to medium-rare), or the nick-and-peek method (see page 19). Salt and pepper the steak before resting for 5 minutes in a warming oven (170°F) or on a warm plate under a loose tent of foil.

To serve, slice the steak and put the pieces on warm plates. Slather a layer of the tapenade on each portion, reserving the remainder to bring to the table. The wild rice and a portion of leafy greens complete the plate.

Wild Rice

Mixes of cultivated wild rice and black or red rice are the most widely available, but the real thing is available from Grey Owl (see the Pantry). Watch the cooking time if you use a blend.

1 cup wild rice

4 cups chicken stock

1 teaspoon kosher salt

2 tablespoons unsalted butter

1 cup cremini mushrooms, trimmed and chopped

Freshly ground black pepper

Combine the rice, stock, and salt in a saucepan with a lid and cook, covered, over low heat for 50 minutes before checking for doneness. The rice will probably need another 10 minutes, but watch it carefully so it doesn't scorch. Add more stock or water if the pot dries out before the rice cooks. When it's done, the rice will be pleasantly chewy with no crunch. When the rice is nearly cooked, melt the butter in a separate sauté pan and add the mushrooms, cooking over high heat until they are slightly crispy on the edges, about 5 minutes. Combine the mushrooms and rice, along with any butter left in the pan. Stir and taste, adding more butter, freshly ground black pepper, or additional salt as needed.

Leafy Greens

Lacinato kale, the noncurly variety, is my favorite—I love its deep green color and pleasantly mineral taste. To prep kale, begin by slicing the leafy green off the stem: hold each leaf and slice along the stem on each side with a long, sharp knife. If you are using Swiss chard or bok choy, the stem is part of the pleasure; just trim the ends and chop the leaves.

2 tablespoons olive oil, plus more for garnish

1 to 2 garlic cloves, peeled and thinly sliced

1 shallot, coarsely chopped

1/2 teaspoon kosher salt

1 large bunch greens such as kale (stemmed), bok choy, or the colorful Swiss chard, coarsely chopped

1/4 cup water

Freshly ground pepper (optional)

Heat the oil over medium heat and add the garlic and shallot. Cook gently, stirring occasionally, for 2 minutes. Add the salt and greens and toss to coat with oil. Add 1/4 cup water, cover, and cook for 5 minutes. Uncover and stir, allowing any remaining water to evaporate, about 2 minutes. Taste for salt. The greens should be tender but still have some backbone. A drizzle of very good olive oil and some fresh black pepper never hurts.

Chunky Winter Braise
with Prunes and Root Vegetables over Buckwheat Dumplings

Making this is like tossing together a big salad that goes in the oven and comes out, an hour later, as a deeply satisfying meal. Next to a buttery heap of Buckwheat Dumplings, this is winter eating at its most elemental. If you're in no mood to make your own dumplings, by all means just buy some broad egg noodles.

Serves 4

OVEN BRAISE

6 carrots, peeled and sliced in half lengthwise and then the lengths in half

2 parsnips, peeled and sliced in half lengthwise and then the lengths in half

3 leeks, lower two-thirds cut into 1/2-inch rounds

1 celery heart with leaves, ribs sliced into 1/2-inch pieces (about 1 cup), leaves and tops chopped and reserved

1 good handful parsley, coarsely chopped

12 or so cremini mushrooms, brushed clean and trimmed

Small bouquet of fresh thyme, tied with a string

2 shallots, peeled and cut in half

10 prunes, pitted and cut in half

2 bay leaves

Freshly ground black pepper

1 pound skirt steak, top blade, or top round, trimmed and cut into 1/2-inch cubes (don't buy it precut)

4 teaspoons kosher salt

Flour for dusting

2 tablespoons butter

1 cup chicken stock (page 26)

2 cups red wine

Freshly grated Parmigiano-Reggiano

Put 3 of the carrots, the parsnips, leeks, celery stalks, half of the parsley, the mushrooms, thyme, shallots, prunes, bay leaves, and a grinding of pepper into a big braising pot. Use whatever you have that is big, fairly deep, wide mouthed, and very heavy. It needs to have a lid.

Preheat the oven to 350°F. After cutting the meat into cubes, give it a dose of 1 teaspoon of the kosher salt and toss with the flour to coat. Heat the butter in a large frying pan and when it's hot, add half the meat. The pieces shouldn't be touching. Let them brown, about 3 minutes per side, over medium-high heat. Once you've done a couple of batches and the meat is crispy and tasty looking on all sides (this isn't about cooking the meat all the way, just caramelizing the exterior), it can all go in your big braising pot along with the vegetables and herbs. While your frying pan is still hot, add the stock and scrape the bottom to loosen all the tasty bits.

Now you have a surprisingly pretty pot full of meat and vegetables ready to come together in the oven. Add the remaining 3 teaspoons of salt and toss before adding the wine and the stock from your frying pan. Cover, put it in the oven, and forget about it for an hour.

After an hour, add the reserved celery leaves, the remaining half of the carrots, and the remaining half of the parsley. Give the whole thing a stir and return the pot to the oven without the lid. Half an hour later it should be ready, with the now tender meat and mushrooms an indistinguishable dark wine color contrasting with bright carrots and bits of green. The parsnips should have caramelized and the prunes melded into the rich sauce. Spoon it out next to a pile of dumplings and add a generous grating of fresh cheese. Don't neglect to finish off that bottle of wine you cooked with—if you haven't already.

Buckwheat Dumplings

Because they are cooked in water and then fried in butter, these dumplings are crispy around the edges—making them hard to resist.

1¼ cups buckwheat flour

1 cup all-purpose unbleached white flour

1 teaspoon kosher salt

Dusting of freshly grated nutmeg

½ teaspoon baking powder

½ cup milk

2 eggs

2 tablespoons unsalted butter

Kosher salt and freshly ground black pepper

Chopped parsley for garnish

Bring a large pot of water (or use chicken stock) to a boil with a good pinch of salt in it. Also set up a colander in the sink. You'll use it to hold the dumplings while you run cold water over them.

Combine the buckwheat and white flours, salt, nutmeg, and baking powder in a bowl. Use a whisk to blend them. In a separate bowl, combine the milk and eggs, and then add them to the dry mixture. No need to treat the batter delicately—it's more a dough than a batter. Once the dough is thoroughly mixed, you'll need to judge how sticky it is. If it's too sticky to handle, add more flour and, with floured hands, turn out onto an immaculate, lightly floured surface. Gently flatten the dough before you begin to pinch off pea-size bits and put them on a plate—the bits of dough won't be round, but they shouldn't be any bigger around than a peanut. When you have a plateful, dump them into the boiling water and cook until they rise to the surface—usually 30 seconds or so.

Using a slotted spoon, scoop out the dumplings and transfer them to the colander. Run cold water over them until they're cool, and then transfer to a bowl to clear the colander for the next batch. Repeat until all the dough is used.

To serve, heat the butter in your largest sauté pan over medium heat. Put the dumplings in the pan, add a generous pinch of salt, and cook for 4 to 6 minutes, or until the dumplings are slightly crispy on the edges. Before tasting one, add a generous grind of black pepper. Add more salt as needed and sprinkle with chopped parsley before serving.

The Julia Burger
with Crispy Onion Rings and Purple Slaw

This burger embodies the Julia Child ethos—a fearless embrace of all things fatty and an unwavering devotion to pleasure. It's inspired by a *Jacques and Julia* rerun. I loved the way she piled everything on to create a monster sandwich worthy of Fred Flintstone. Julia didn't ask people to grind their own steak, but it makes good sense these days. Don't be put off by the idea of putting a steak in the food processor. It just takes a minute and you end up with a really terrific-tasting burger. Finally, don't wuss out on the condiments and accompaniments. Your burger goes like this: toasted roll, butter, mayo, ketchup, meat with melted cheese, bacon, lettuce, tomato, onion. Try it once. Crispy Onion Rings go great with this burger, as does Purple Slaw.

Serves 4

GRILL OR PAN-FRY

1¹/₂ pounds steak (hangar, top blade, skirt, sirloin—whatever you like and can afford), trimmed of all visible fat and cut into 2-inch chunks

1¹/₂ teaspoons kosher salt

Freshly ground black pepper

1 to 2 tablespoons peanut oil for pan-frying

8 slices bacon, cooked crisp

1 tomato, sliced

4 lettuce leaves, cleaned

4 fresh Kaiser rolls, toasted and buttered

4 slices sharp Cheddar cheese

Mayonnaise

Ketchup

4 thin slices raw onion (I admit, I pass on these)

Put the cut-up pieces of steak in the food processor along with the salt and a good grind of black pepper and pulse a few times—just long enough so the meat will hold together and there aren't any big chunks left. Pick out any visible strands of white gristle. Gently form 4 patties, neither pressing nor squeezing the meat. Air is good. You should have about ¹/₃-pound burgers, which suits the no-holds-barred spirit of this meal. Very thick patties are more difficult to cook; make them thinner—1¹/₂ inches is about right—and cook them fast and hot.

Before you cook your burgers, make sure the bacon is done to a crisp and that you have a tomato sliced, lettuce washed, and Kaiser rolls toasting. Butter each roll while it's hot. When everything is ready, cook the burgers either on a grill or in a cast-iron pan. Whichever method you choose, don't press the burgers down with your spatula as you cook! And don't forget to put the cheese on for the last 2 to 3 minutes of cooking on the second side. This should give it time to melt.

To grill, your coals should be so hot that you can comfortably keep your hand 2 inches above the grate for 3 seconds—just! (For gas grills, this means 450°F.) Make sure the grill is well oiled. Put the burgers on the hottest part of the grill and sear for 3 to 5 minutes on each side. If they're browning too much, move them to a cooler part of the grill to finish cooking. **To pan-fry,** heat the peanut oil in a heavy pan until it's very hot—almost smoking. Sear the burgers for 3 minutes on each side over high heat before turning down the burner. Finish cooking over moderate heat, flipping the burgers every few minutes as they cook.

I like a rare burger. However you cook your burgers, test for doneness often by poking, or use an instant-read thermometer. Take them off at between 125° and 130°F for rare to medium-rare. Like a steak, a burger needs to rest in the warming oven (170°F) or on a warm plate under a loose tent of foil before you serve it—3 minutes should do it.

Let the buttered rolls cool a little before putting a smear of mayonnaise and an even thinner smear of ketchup on each side. Put the cooked burger on the bun, add the bacon to cover the meat and enough lettuce to do the same. Add a slice of tomato and a slice of raw onion before putting the top on. Eat.

Crispy Onion Rings

1¹/₂ cups cornmeal

1¹/₂ cups flour

¹/₄ teaspoon cayenne

¹/₂ teaspoon kosher salt, plus more for sprinkling

3 onions (Vidalia or red onions are best)

3 to 4 cups whole milk to cover the onions

6 cups peanut or vegetable oil, or at least 3 inches in a pot

Combine the cornmeal, flour, cayenne, and ¹/₂ teaspoon salt in a shallow bowl and set aside.

Slice the onions as thin as you can using a mandoline or your sharpest knife. Drop the slices into a bowl and cover with milk. This soaking removes some of the bite, making them sweeter and more mellow. Let the onions sit out on the counter until you're ready to cook them. An hour in the milk is ideal.

In a fryer or in a large stockpot, heat the oil until it reaches 350°F. If you don't have a thermometer, test the oil by tossing in a piece of onion to see whether it really sizzles. It should.

When your oil is hot and your burger is just about ready, remove the slices from the milk and douse the onions in the cornmeal-flour mixture, coating evenly. Working in manageable batches, cook the onion rings until they are a toasty brown, about 5 minutes depending on the temperature of your oil. Remove to a wire rack set over a plate or to a colander and sprinkle with kosher salt. Keep them hot in a warming oven (170°F).

Purple Slaw

In summer, slaw goes with everything that comes off the grill. Use white cabbage if you prefer, or mix in radishes, jicama, kohlrabi, or carrots. If you like your slaw on the sweet side, whisk a little honey or raw sugar into the dressing.

1 medium head purple cabbage, cored

1 shallot

3/4 cup Homemade Dressing (page 118) or 1/2 cup mayonnaise combined with 2 tablespoons apple cider vinegar and 1 egg yolk

1/2 teaspoon kosher salt

Freshly ground black pepper

Shred the cabbage and the shallot together; I use the food processor for both. You should end up with 5 to 6 cups of shredded cabbage. Once that's done, combine with the Homemade Dressing in a big, wide bowl and mix until the dressing has coated the cabbage. Taste for seasoning. I like mine peppery and salty.

CHAPTER TWO
Bistro Steak

This chapter covers many of the world's classic preparations. Bistro food is less about innovation than it is about retaining the integrity of origins. Think butter, cream, shallots, fresh herbs, and, of course, wine. The flavors you're in for are subtle but distinctive. Whether it's Filet Béarnaise (page 115), Montpelier Butter on Rib Steak (page 74), or the classic Steak au Poivre (page 109), don't think you've had and know it. There's a lot of dumbed-down food out there, and classics are the first to come in for this treatment. By sticking with fresh ingredients while keeping the cooking as easy as possible, each one of these recipes evokes simple refinement.

With one exception, the kitchen necessities for this chapter are really just the staples of a solid American kitchen: great olive oil, fresh sweet butter, good wine vinegars, non-ultrapasteurized heavy cream, and plenty of fresh produce. The one item I call for here that will cause you trouble is the chicken juices. Having some of this stuff around in the freezer will turn your sauces from good to great (see my note on making it on page 22). Sure, the sauces here are the most challenging in the book, but that's not to say they're difficult. Don't be cowed by all the hype you hear about how hard it is to make a sauce. Anyone, given the ingredients, can make even the most challenging sauce here.

Nibbles, Starters, and Sweets

If you're putting together a full menu for guests—with a first course, main course, cheeses, and dessert—stick to the classics when you're looking for something to nibble on with wine or cocktails before dinner. As much as I love them, cheese and paté are too heavy before a dinner of steak; great olives, crackers, fresh nuts, and salted, crunchy radishes have much greater appeal. If you want to be more ambitious, put out some smoked trout or salmon with a little crème fraîche, dill, and a few capers on top. Cured fish is always better if you happen to be pouring champagne, too.

To start your meal, a soup is easy to do ahead and always elegant. Of course, cold soup in summer is one of the pleasures of hot weather—I find gazpacho unpalatable and vichyssoise divine. Salads are fine as starters if you don't plan to have one after the meal, as the French traditionally do. Frisée aux Lardons is one of the great, traditional salads. Despite the richness of the poached egg on top, I often serve it as a first course. An authentic Ceasar salad, made with raw egg yolks and plenty of anchovies, is also a great way to get your meal going.

Rather than doing anything fussy, like a formal cheese course after the meal, consider getting one or two perfectly ripe cheeses along with a loaf of fresh walnut bread. Put the cheese and bread out on the table with Herb Salad (page 119). This blends the cheese and salad courses effortlessly into one another while giving the hosts time to think about dessert.

Great fruit, whether it's Medjool dates, figs, or perfect berries, are an elegant end to a rich meal. Something light is often all you need after a meal of steak, sides, cheese, and salad. But sometimes overindulgence calls for even greater excess—if so, you'll never be sorry to have a crême brulée, a fresh fruit tart, or even a slice of vanilla génoise cake with just a gloss of butter cream. Whatever you decide, espresso and a glass of Muscat de Beaumes-de-Venise never hurt anyone after a great meal.

Drinks

French and Italian wines have lately been overrun by those from newer wine producing countries. From California to Australia and from Chile to New Zealand, these regions are bigger players than ever in the wine industry. When you're making a recipe from this chapter, think about going with a traditional wine. What about a great Côtes du Rhône or a French Bordeaux? Don't forget about those incredible Italian Barolos and Barbarescos either. Drink what you like, but if you're eating old-world food, I think it makes sense to drink wine from the same part of the world.

Montpelier Butter on Rib Steak
with Mixed Orzo, Beets, and Cranberry Beans

This butter has been around for well over a hundred years, and when you taste it, you'll see why. Combining raw and cooked eggs, anchovies, and, of course, butter with a potent dose of herbs and watercress makes it big and memorable. Warm it up with Mixed Orzo, Beets, and Cranberry Beans—showy but earthy-tasting vegetables set off by a creamy white goat cheese. The cheese, just slightly melted, is a surprise—soft, warm, and goaty.

Serves 4

GRILL OR PAN-FRY

4 rib steaks, bone-in or boneless

1 teaspoon kosher salt

Oil for rubbing

1 to 2 tablespoons peanut oil for pan-frying

MONTPELIER BUTTER

3 tarragon leaves

1/2 bunch watercress (1 cup leaves)

1 tablespoon parsley, chopped

3 spinach leaves (6 if baby spinach)

3 whole chives

1 shallot, chopped

2 hard-boiled egg yolks

1 teaspoon of your best white wine vinegar

1/4 cup chervil tops, chopped

4 tablespoons unsalted butter

1 small clove garlic (use 1/2 a clove if in doubt)

2 anchovy filets, drained

Dash of cayenne pepper

Freshly ground pepper

1 raw egg yolk

3 tablespoons olive oil

Prepare the steaks by salting them, and then let them come to room temperature. Rub all over with olive oil just before cooking.

Fill a pot with water and bring it to a boil. Dump the tarragon, watercress, parsley, spinach, chives, and shallot in the boiling water. Leave them there for 1 minute, and then drain the pot's contents through a fine sieve. Shock the herbs by running cold water over them—this stops the cooking and preserves their vivid color. Now, dry the herbs thoroughly by wrapping them in a clean dish towel and squeezing. When they emerge from the towel, you should have a bright green, densely packed disc in your hands. Put it in the food processor along with the remaining ingredients except the olive oil (a mortar and pestle works, too). Pulse until well blended and then add the olive oil slowly. Blend thoroughly. "Let it be observed," as George Augustus Sala writes in 1896 about this butter in *The Thorough Good Cook*, "that no flavor should predominate." Taste and judge for yourself.

To grill, your coals should be so hot that you can comfortably keep your hand 2 inches above the grate for 3 seconds—just! (For gas grills, this means 450°F.) Put the oiled steaks on the hottest part of the grill and sear for 3 to 5 minutes on each side before you begin to fuss over them. That means moving the steaks to a cooler part of the grill, flipping, poking, and watching as you work toward crispy-brown perfection for another 8 to 12 minutes. **To pan-fry,** heat the peanut oil in a heavy pan until it's very hot—almost smoking. Sear the steaks for 3 minutes on each side over high heat before turning down the burner. Cook over moderate heat for an additional 8 to 12 minutes, turning the steaks every few minutes as they slowly brown. For steaks more than 2 inches thick, you may want to finish cooking them by putting them, pan and all, in a 400°F oven.

However you cook your steaks, check for doneness often, using the finger-poke method, an instant-read thermometer (120° to 130°F for rare to medium-rare), or the nick-and-peek method (see page 19). After cooking, rest the steaks in a warming oven (170°F) or on a warm plate under a loose tent of foil for 5 minutes.

Put the steaks on warm plates along with a scoop of the mixed orzo, beets, and beans. Before bringing it all to the table, spread the butter lavishly on your steak.

Mixed Orzo, Beets, and Cranberry Beans

Capri is a super-fresh goat cheese made by Westfield Farm, just outside Boston. It's incredible! Substitute any good, not-too-salty, young goat cheese. Out West, Laura Chenel makes an excellent fresh goat cheese called Chef's Chèvre that would be perfect.

2 pounds beets, quartered and then cut into 1/2-inch slices

1 cup fresh cranberry beans or fresh or frozen edamame

2 tablespoons your best olive oil

1 teaspoon kosher salt, plus more for garnish

2 cups orzo

5 ounces Capri or other young goat cheese (about 1/2 cup)

Freshly ground black pepper

Set up a steamer basket in a heavy saucepan with a lid. Put the beets in the steamer basket and cook, covered, for 5 minutes. Add the cranberry beans and steam for another 5 to 8 minutes. Test both a bean and a beet; they should be nearly tender but still firm. Drain and transfer the vegetables to a bowl and toss with 1 tablespoon of the olive oil.

Bring a large pot of salted water to a boil and add the orzo. Cook for 8 to 10 minutes, or according to package directions. Drain and return the pasta to the pot. Toss with the remaining 1 tablespoon olive oil. Taste and add salt as needed.

To serve, the orzo, beets, and beans should be warm but no longer hot. Transfer the orzo to a large shallow bowl. Put the beets and beans on top of the orzo and sprinkle on the cheese. The cheese should soften and warm a little on the vegetables. A grind of fresh black pepper finishes it.

Strip Steak with Sautéed Morels,
Thyme Twigs, and White Beans

Morels or chanterelles? It's a tough call when it comes to deciding which of these mushroom varieties is my favorite. Chanterelles, of course, are the most delicately flavored—as much like perfume as food. The apricot-colored flutes need gentle handling and subtle accompaniments. Morels, on the other hand, are hardier, with their thick stems and big porous pockets. Tasting more of the earth and forest than of anything else, morels can stand up next to a few herbs and a steak all on their own. That's what this recipe is about: tasting the mushrooms, with the white beans, rich strip steak, and thyme.

Serves 4

GRILL OR PAN-FRY

4 strip steaks

1 teaspoon kosher salt

Olive oil for rubbing

1 to 2 tablespoons peanut oil for pan-frying

1 pound fresh morels (or substitute 3 to 4 ounces dried morels)

3 tablespoons unsalted butter

Kosher salt and freshly ground black pepper

6 sprigs fresh thyme (reserve 4 for garnish)

Prepare your steaks by salting them and then let them come to room temperature. Rub them with olive oil just before cooking.

Clean the mushrooms gently with a towel or a brush. (Don't wash them.) Trim off the ends of the stems and slice the larger mushrooms in half lengthwise. Discard any mushrooms that are moldy, mushy, or slimy. Fresh morels should feel dry to the touch. Ideally, they shouldn't be very dirty, either. Don't obsess. While you don't want them gritty, a little of the forest floor isn't going to kill you. (If you're reconstituting dried mushrooms, just cover with boiling water or, even better, with stock, an hour before using and then drain them carefully on a paper towel.)

In a heavy frying pan, melt the butter over medium heat. Add the mushrooms and allow them to brown and the butter to be absorbed before adding the salt. Salt makes the mushrooms release some of their moisture. You want them to sauté and brown around the edges, not to stew in a mess of butter and their own juices; turn up the heat if there's too much liquid in the pan. The mushrooms are done when they have slightly crispy edges and have lost their raw, porous quality. This takes 7 to 10 minutes. Remove to a warm oven (170°F) when done—but don't leave them there too long. They'll shrivel and dry out.

Start your steaks while the mushrooms are cooking. **To grill,** your coals should be so hot that you can comfortably keep your hand 2 inches above the grate for 3 seconds—just! (For gas grills, this means 450°F.) Put the oiled steaks on the hottest part of the grill and sear for 3 to 5 minutes on each side before you begin to fuss over them. That means moving the steaks to a cooler part of the grill and cooking more gently for 6 to 10 minutes, flipping, poking, and watching as you work toward crispy-brown perfection. **To pan-fry,** heat the peanut oil in a heavy pan until it's very hot—almost smoking. Sear the steaks for 3 minutes on each side over high heat before turning down the burner. Cook over moderate heat for an additional 6 to 10 minutes, turning the steaks every few minutes as they slowly brown. If your kitchen is filling with smoke, put the steaks, pan and all, in a 400°F oven to finish cooking.

However you cook your steaks, check for doneness often, using the finger-poke method, an instant-read thermometer (120° to 130°F for rare to medium-rare), or the nick-and-peek method (see page 19). Generously salt and pepper each steak before resting them in the warming oven (170°F) or on a warm plate under a loose tent of foil for 5 minutes.

When everything is ready and the meat has rested, place a steak on each plate alongside some beans. Portion out the mushrooms on top of the steaks, with some scattered on the plate. To finish, strip 2 sprigs of thyme among the 4 plates, allowing the tiny leaves to fall over the mushrooms, beans, and the steak. Finally, place a sprig of thyme across each steak and serve.

White Beans

1½ cups dried white beans (look for flageolet, navy, great Northern, pea beans, or cannellini—any will do, even though the flageolet are the most traditional)

2 cloves garlic, crushed

3 sprigs of thyme

2 ribs celery, whole

1 carrot, cut in half lengthwise

1 bay leaf

¼ cup olive oil

6 cups chicken stock (page 26)

3 pieces bacon, cut into bite-size pieces

2 large leeks, sliced into rounds

1 teaspoon kosher salt

Freshly ground black pepper

Making the beans takes a while—up to 4 hours—so plan ahead. If you're organized, you can save time by soaking the dried beans in water overnight. Also, don't use salted stock or add salt before the beans are cooked, since it will make them take longer.

Rinse and drain the beans if you've soaked them. Stir the beans, garlic, thyme, celery, carrot, and bay leaf in the olive oil in a heavy pot over medium heat. Let everything soften a little without scorching. Add enough stock to cover the beans generously and bring the mixture to a simmer. Skim after 5 minutes. Let the beans cook, adding more stock as needed until you've used it all and then water, as necessary. After 2 to 3 hours, when the beans are tender but still firm, cook the bacon pieces until crisp in a heavy cast-iron pan, drain the fat, and add the bacon to the beans.

Reserve the pan you cooked the bacon in, pouring off most of the grease, but still leaving a nice slick of it, along with any tasty bits. Cook the leeks in the same pan until soft, about 5 minutes, before adding them to the beans. Remove the spent thyme sprigs and the bay leaves, if you can find them. Taste and add salt and pepper to adjust the seasoning.

Porterhouse with Herb Butter,
Slow-Roasted Garlic, and Creamed Spinach

This herb butter is in my food pantheon. Something about the combination of sweet butter, thyme, and shallot with the salty, rich meat sends me into bliss mode. I like to use all the herbs I've listed below when I have them growing in my garden. In winter, when I have to buy herbs, I might not use as many kinds. Don't forget to squeeze out a clove of sweet, roasted garlic between bites of Creamed Spinach. As always, Grilled Bread (page 119) would be a welcome, crunchy addition.

Serves 4

GRILL OR PAN-FRY

1 large porterhouse (about 2 pounds of any steak will work here)

1 teaspoon kosher salt

Olive oil for rubbing

1 to 2 tablespoons peanut oil for pan-frying

HERB BUTTER

4 tablespoons unsalted butter

1 shallot, minced

3 tablespoons herbs, chopped (tarragon, thyme, parsley, basil, chives)

1/2 teaspoon kosher salt

Freshly ground black pepper

Prepare the steak by salting it, and then let it come to room temperature. Rub with a bit of olive oil just before cooking.

To make the herb butter, mash the butter, shallot, herbs, salt, and pepper together until smooth—it should look like savory, green-flecked frosting. There's no need to fuss with it further by shaping it into a log or any other fancy preparation; it just gets smeared, still soft, on the steak.

To grill, your coals should be so hot that you can comfortably keep your hand 2 inches above the grate for 3 seconds—just! (For gas grills, this means 450°F.) Put the oiled steak on the hottest part of the grill and sear for 3 to 5 minutes on each side before you begin to fuss over it. That means moving the steak to a cooler part of the grill and cooking for an additional 8 to 12 minutes, flipping, poking, and watching as you work toward crispy-brown perfection. **To pan-fry,** heat the peanut oil in a heavy pan until it's very hot—almost smoking. Sear the steak for 3 minutes on each side over high heat before turning down the burner. Cook for an additional 8 to 12 minutes over moderate heat, turning the steak every few minutes as it slowly browns. For very thick steak, put it, pan and all, in a 400°F oven to finish cooking.

However you cook your steak, check for doneness often, using the finger-poke method, an instant-read thermometer (120° to 130°F for rare to medium-rare), or the nick-and-peek method (see page 19). Generously salt and pepper the steak and smear on half of the herb butter before resting it in the warming oven (170°F) for 5 minutes.

To serve, slice the steak so each piece has some of the filet and some of the loin and put it on warm plates with the Slow-Roasted Garlic and Creamed Spinach. Pour any juices that may have run off the steak while it rested over each steak and then top with another dollop of herb butter.

Slow-Roasted Garlic

Buy the freshest garlic you can find from a good source. Most important, look at where it was grown. I don't like Chinese garlic; grown for a long shelf life, easy shipping, and productivity, it hardly has any flavor. Do a taste test. You'll be amazed.

4 heads garlic

Olive oil

Kosher salt

Preheat the oven to 300°F. Smash the garlic heads with the palm of your hand to break the cloves apart. Remove the outer paper from the garlic but leave the skin on. In a roasting pan, toss the garlic cloves with a drizzle of olive oil and a pinch of salt. Roast for half an hour. They should turn brown around the edges; the real test of doneness is squeezing the soft, mellow flesh into your mouth.

Creamed Spinach

Use fresh, full-grown spinach and non-ultrapasteurized cream for the best flavor. For very large leaves of spinach, use a sharp knife to slice off the leaves from either side of the stem. For smaller, more tender leaves, just trim off the coarse stems.

2 large heads mature spinach, stemmed and rinsed (4 to 5 cups, tightly packed)

1/2 cup heavy cream

1 teaspoon kosher salt

Freshly ground black pepper

Stuff the spinach into a pot big enough to hold it with the cover on tight. Turn the heat to medium-high and let the spinach heat up. There's no need to add water; the water on the leaves from rinsing is enough to steam the leaves. The spinach should be wilted and ready to come out in 3 minutes.

Drain any water from the pot and allow the spinach to cool. Use a big clean towel to squeeze out any remaining water. Put the dried, pressed spinach on a cutting board, chop it, and set it aside.

Return the spinach pot (without the spinach in it) to the stove and pour in the cream. Scald the cream (heat it to *almost* boiling), and then add the chopped spinach. Cook over medium heat for 3 to 6 minutes to reduce the cream by half. Add the salt and a good grind of pepper. Taste and adjust for salt.

You can, of course, add a sprinkling of crispy, chopped bacon. It always tastes good.

Strip Steak with Mashed Garlic
and Beets with Their Greens

This combination is the kind of clean, bright food I can't get enough of. Run the beets around in the mashed garlic. Be sure to make up some Grilled Bread (page 119); it's second only to the steak as a vehicle for the mashed garlic.

Serves 4

GRILL OR PAN-FRY

4 strip steaks

1 teaspoon kosher salt

Olive oil for rubbing

3 heads garlic, paper removed and broken apart, skin on

1 to 2 cups chicken stock (page 26)

1 teaspoon kosher salt

1 tablespoon unsalted butter

1 to 2 tablespoons peanut oil for pan-frying

Freshly ground black pepper

Prepare your steaks by salting them, and then let them come to room temperature. Rub with olive oil just before cooking.

In a medium-size saucepan, add the garlic and enough stock to cover. Simmer, covered, over medium heat for 25 minutes. When the time's up, remove the pan from the heat and allow it to cool. Once the cloves are cool enough to handle, pop each out of its skin. Discard the skins and fish around in the stock for any remaining bits of skin that may have fallen off during cooking. Add the salt and butter to the mixture in the pan, then transfer to a blender or food processor. Blend briefly, leaving a little texture. Taste for seasoning and set aside.

To grill, your coals should be so hot that you can comfortably keep your hand 2 inches above the grate for 3 seconds—just! (For gas grills this means 450°F.) Put the oiled steaks on the hottest part of the grill and sear for 3 to 5 minutes on each side over intense heat before you start to fuss over them. That means moving the steaks to a cooler part of the grill and cooking gently over moderate heat for an additional 6 to 10 minutes, flipping, poking, and watching as you work toward crispy-brown perfection. **To pan-fry,** heat the peanut oil in a heavy pan until it's very hot—almost smoking. Sear the steaks for 3 minutes on each side over high heat before turning down the burner. Cook over moderate heat for an additional 6 to 10 minutes, turning the steaks every few minutes as they slowly brown. For steaks more than 2 inches thick, you may want to put them, pan and all, in a 400°F oven to finish cooking.

However you cook your steak, check for doneness often, using the finger-poke method, an instant-read thermometer (120° to 130°F for rare to medium rare), or the nick-and-peek method (see page 19). Generously salt and pepper each steak before resting them in the warming oven (170°F) or on a warm plate under a loose tent of foil for 5 minutes.

Put each steak on a warm plate with the Beets with Their Greens. Smear a generous layer of the garlic puree on each steak and rush everything to the table, good and hot.

Beets with Their Greens

I use lots of beets in my kitchen—they are gorgeous and versatile. Most people are after only the root bulb. This recipe addresses my angst at so wastefully chucking some of the best parts in pursuit of the obvious. Virtually unadorned, except for salt and olive oil, what you end up with is the integral earthy sweetness of a nearly perfect vegetable.

3 beets, with stems and leaves

$1/2$ cup water

2 tablespoons good olive oil

$1/2$ teaspoon kosher salt

Thoroughly wash each beet, using a soft brush if needed. Trim the ends, removing the feathery root tips. Slice the bulb from the tough area where the bulb meets the green stems. Set the greens aside. Trim off any dark or rough areas where the root has been exposed to the light while growing. Using a sharp knife and starting at the top, slice each bulb into $1/2$-inch-thick rounds.

Lay the beet slices flat (they may overlap) in a large frying pan over medium heat. Add the water, cover, and cook for 5 minutes.

While the beets cook, slice the remaining stems and greens by grasping a bunch of them and working from the stem up, cutting in $1/2$-inch increments. Go to the tips of the leaves, roughly chopping the remaining leaf tips. Add the chopped stems and leaves, olive oil, and salt to the pan with the cooking beets. Stir to coat with the oil. Cook, covered, for an additional 5 minutes. Check frequently to be certain the pan doesn't dry out. (The cooking time will depend on the size of the beets; baby beets, if you're lucky enough to find them, can cook whole without precooking the bulb.)

When the time is up, remove the lid and cook off most of the remaining water. Test for doneness. The leaves, stems, and roots should be just tender. Taste for salt and give the whole mixture a final drizzle of your best olive oil.

Rib Eye Marchand de Vins,
Mashed Potatoes, and Asparagus Tips with Shaved Manchego

The French are famous for this kind of sauce: a pan reduction with flavor coming from classic ingredients—shallots, rich stock, thyme, and wine, of course. Use a red you would happily drink, not the bottle you opened and decided to cook with because you hated it. In the spirit of the sauce, I like to use a French Côtes du Rhône. Mashed Potatoes and red wine sauce are a natural together. The Asparagus Tips with Shaved Manchego are a refreshing addition to the meal.

Serves 4

PAN-FRY

4 rib-eye steaks

1 teaspoon kosher salt

Olive oil for rubbing

2 tablespoons peanut oil for pan-frying

Freshly ground black pepper

MARCHAND DE VINS

3 tablespoons unsalted butter

1 large shallot, chopped (2 to 3 tablespoons)

3 sprigs of thyme

3 tablespoons chicken juices (see page 22) or 1/2 cup chicken stock (page 26)

1 1/2 cups red wine (half a bottle)

3 sprigs of parsley

Kosher salt and freshly ground black pepper

Prepare the steaks by salting them, and then let them come to room temperature. Rub with a bit of olive oil just before cooking.

Heat the peanut oil in a heavy pan until it's very hot—almost smoking. Sear the steaks for 3 to 5 minutes on each side over high heat before turning down the burner. Cook for an additional 8 to 12 minutes over moderate heat, turning the steaks every few minutes as they slowly brown. Try not to burn the bottom of the pan, despite the high heat, since you will be using it to make your sauce. Put the steak, pan and all, in a 400°F oven to finish cooking.

Check for doneness after 3 minutes using the finger-poke method, an instant-read thermometer (120° to 130°F for rare to medium-rare), or the nick-and-peek method (see page 19). Generously salt and pepper each steak before resting them on a warm plate under a loose tent of foil for 5 minutes.

Without washing the pan, add the butter, shallots, and thyme sprigs. Cook to soften, scraping the pan with a wooden spoon. After the shallots have softened (2 to 3 minutes), add the chicken juices, continuing to stir and scrape as you work. Before the sauce begins to really cook, add the wine. Let it simmer as it reduces by half, 8 to 15 minutes. Finish with salt and black pepper to taste.

Slice the steak and arrange it on a warm platter with the asparagus. Sprinkle with parsley and serve. The potatoes can come out to the table in a warm bowl of their own.

Mashed Potatoes

Going a little overboard with the scalded milk, butter, and salt is what makes truly great mashed potatoes. Don't even try to pretend these are good for you.

3 pounds potatoes (Yukon Gold are my favorite)

1 cup whole milk

1/2 cup heavy cream

1 1/2 teaspoons salt

4 tablespoons unsalted butter

Freshly ground black pepper

Cut the potatoes into even chunks for cooking. Peel them first if you like, but make sure they're clean. I use organic potatoes and skip the peeling.

Set up a steamer basket in a large pot with a lid, with water just coming through the holes of the steamer, and cook the potatoes in it over medium heat. After 15 minutes test for doneness with a fork. A done potato will split or yield to the fork easily. A potato that needs more time will stop the fork or at least give it some resistance. You could also pop one in your mouth.

When they've cooked through, drain and return to the same pot sans steamer. In a separate pot over medium heat, combine the milk and cream. Heat the mixture just until a skin forms on the surface. Once you see that wrinkly scum, dump the mixture in with the potatoes, add the salt, butter, and some black pepper. Mash, but don't work the potatoes more than you need to. Depending on the variety, mashing can make them turn gluey. Taste for seasoning and cover to keep warm. Reheat gently before serving, if necessary. Mashed potatoes should be served piping hot.

Asparagus Tips with Shaved Manchego

Buy your asparagus when it isn't coming from too far away; it should snap with freshness when you bend it. Manchego is a Spanish sheep's milk cheese that's become popular in recent years. Look for raw milk Manchego that's been aged for a year—it's really good.

2 pounds asparagus

3 tablespoons unsalted butter

1/2 teaspoon kosher salt

1/4 pound Manchego cheese, shaved with a vegetable peeler

To prepare the asparagus, grasp each one by the end and bend. The asparagus should snap in half just above the center. If the asparagus bends all the way around, refusing to snap, get rid of it. Repeat until you have a nice pile of tips with a little stalk.

In a large sauté pan, heat the butter over medium-high heat until melted. Add the asparagus, salt them, and cook for 3 to 7 minutes, stirring frequently. The pan should be very hot but the butter should not smoke; turn down the heat if it does. How long the asparagus take to cook depends on how thick they are. Taste them frequently and transfer them to a large plate when they are just tender but still a little crunchy. Transfer to a warm platter and pile on shavings of Manchego to cover the top. Be generous. I don't like to add black pepper to this dish; it's a distraction.

Skirt Steak with Harissa,
Blackened Sweet Pepper Couscous, and Carrot-Cumin Salad

Harissa is a staple of Tunisia. It's here with the bistro recipes because Tunisia, like Morocco and Algeria, engaged in centuries of trade, occupation, and migration with Europe, resulting in a genuine cross-fertilization of flavors and ingredients. To make a sauce that will give you a nice slow burn, but is still mellow enough that you can taste the cumin, coriander, and caraway—not to mention the meat itself—use fresh serrano chiles. The Blackened Sweet Pepper Couscous soaks up the sauce, while the Carrot-Cumin Salad cools things off.

Serves 4

GRILL OR PAN-FRY

2 pounds skirt steak

1 teaspoon kosher salt

Olive oil for rubbing

1 to 2 tablespoons peanut oil for pan-frying

HARISSA

1/2 cup butter

3 serrano chiles, halved and seeded

1 red or orange bell pepper, halved and seeded

Olive oil

2 cloves garlic, peeled and crushed

1 teaspoon kosher salt

1 teaspoon cumin seeds

1 teaspoon caraway seeds

1 teaspoon whole coriander

3 tablespoons lemon juice

Mint leaves, coarsely chopped, for garnish

Prepare the steak by salting it, and then let it come to room temperature. Rub with olive oil before cooking.

To make the harissa, clarify the butter by melting it slowly in a small pot over very low heat—it should not brown. Once it has simmered for several minutes, most of the milk solids will sink and a skin will form on top once the water has fully evaporated. Skim off and discard any cloudy or foamy liquid from the top, then pour off the clear butter slowly. Stop pouring when you reach the milky-white sediment, which you will also discard. Measure out 1/3 cup of the translucent yellow liquid and set aside.

Preheat the oven to 450°F. Smear the chiles and bell pepper with oil inside and out and roast for 10 minutes, or until the chiles and pepper begin to brown on the bottom and blister on the top. Remove from the oven and set aside to cool. Once cool, peel the skins from the flesh, then chop the flesh and set aside.

Crush the garlic and salt in a mortar to form a paste (if you prefer, you can use a food processor). Toast the cumin and caraway seeds in a dry pan over medium heat until fragrant and then add them, along with the whole coriander, to the garlic mixture. Put the spice-garlic mixture in a food processor with the chopped chiles and bell pepper. Pulse, then add the lemon juice. Finally, with the machine on, slowly pour in the clarified butter. As the butter cools the sauce will stiffen. Taste for salt and heat.

To grill, your coals should be so hot that you can comfortably keep your hand 2 inches above the grate for 3 seconds—just! (For gas grills, this means 450°F.) Put the oiled steak on the hottest part of the grill and sear for 3 to 5 minutes on each side over high heat before you begin to fuss over it. That means moving the steak to a cooler part of the grill and cooking it for at most 2 to 5 minutes more—it should always be rare! **To pan-fry,** heat the peanut oil in your heaviest pan until it's very hot—almost smoking. Sear the steak for 3 minutes on each side over high heat before turning down the burner. Cook over moderate heat for at most 2 to 5 minutes more, turning the steak often as it slowly browns.

However you cook your steak, check for doneness often, using the finger-poke method, an instant-read thermometer (120° to 130°F for rare to medium-rare), or the nick-and-peek method (see page 19). After cooking, rest the steak in a warming oven (170°F) or on a warm plate under a loose tent of foil for 5 minutes.

To serve, slice the steak against the grain, creating long, thin pieces. Divide the steak among the individual plates and smear the sliced steak with some of the harissa. Scatter each plate with the mint, place the steak in the middle, pile some couscous next to it, and spoon on some Carrot-Cumin Salad.

Blackened Sweet Pepper Couscous

Use the big pearls of couscous, the Israeli variety, if you can find them.

1 red bell pepper, halved and seeded

1 orange bell pepper, halved and seeded

Olive oil for roasting

2 tablespoons butter

1 cup couscous

2 cups boiling water

1 teaspoon kosher salt

Preheat the oven to 450°F. Coat the peppers with olive oil and roast them in the oven for 10 minutes, or until they begin to blacken on the bottom and blister on top. Set aside to cool.

Melt the butter in a heavy saucepan and add the couscous. Cook, stirring frequently, over medium heat until you begin to smell it cooking—the aroma is a bit like roasting grain. Add the boiling water and the salt, stirring as you go. Turn down the heat, cover, and simmer for 10 minutes, or until the water has evaporated and the pearls are tender.

Slice the peppers into short, thin strips, about 1 inch long. Toss the peppers in with the couscous, as well as a little extra butter or olive oil if you're feeling the need. Taste for salt.

Carrot-Cumin Salad

Use the best carrots you can find. They should have fresh-looking tops still on. Whole, freshly roasted cumin—not ground—makes a big difference.

8 carrots, peeled and grated (3 cups)

1/4 teaspoon salt

1 tablespoon good olive oil

Squeeze of lemon

1 teaspoon whole cumin seeds

Combine the carrots in a bowl with the salt, olive oil, and lemon (squeeze the lemon gently, you don't want much). Toast the cumin seeds in a small frying pan (not nonstick) until they are fragrant and just beginning to color. Grind the toasted seeds with a mortar and pestle or in a spice grinder, leaving some just crushed and others pulverized. Add to the carrot mixture and toss. Taste for salt and serve.

Shallot and Sherry Vinegar–Marinated Flank Steak with Sautéed Wild Mushrooms and Robinson Bar Potatoes

I have great memories of tagging along with my parents on mushroom hunting trips. We'd head up Hunter Mountain, in Aspen, where the trees provided the perfect loamy, damp soil for chanterelles. In other spots, like under the cottonwood trees in the valley, we'd hunt morels, boletus, and suillis. Today I buy them for—yikes—$60 a pound at Whole Foods or Dean & Deluca. Times clearly have changed. If you live on the West Coast, you might have better luck finding these beauties at a more approachable price. If so, pile them on. Steak with mushrooms is a classic combination. The Robinson Bar Potatoes keeps this far from spartan.

Chanterelle, porcini (also known as cépes in France and boletus in the United States), and morels are my favorites because they have such great flavor. In a pinch, you can use plain old white or brown field mushrooms, but you might want to goose them up by adding some shiitakes.

Serves 4

GRILL OR PAN-FRY

2 shallots, minced (3 to 4 tablespoons)

1 teaspoon kosher salt

3 tablespoons sherry vinegar

2 pounds flank steak

Olive oil for rubbing

1 to 2 tablespoons peanut oil for pan-frying

Freshly ground black pepper

Maldon salt

SAUTÉED WILD MUSHROOMS

1 pound wild mushrooms or 3 ounces dried mushrooms

3 tablespoons unsalted butter

1 teaspoon kosher salt

In a shallow glass dish, combine the shallots, salt, and vinegar. Add the steak to the dish and marinate for at least an hour on the counter or for up to 24 hours in the refrigerator. Before cooking, let the steak come to room temperature and remove as much of the marinade as you can, then rub it with olive oil.

Prepare the mushrooms by judiciously trimming their ends and rubbing them clean. Don't wash them—water does no favors to any mushroom. Once the mushrooms are clean, slice the larger ones, leaving whole any that are bite-size. Heat a large, heavy frying pan. Add the butter and when it begins to brown around the edges, add the mushrooms. I like to cook my mushrooms hot. Let them brown on the edges but don't let the pan dry out completely. They'll absorb a lot of butter if you let them. When the pan does dry out, rather than adding more butter, add the salt. This will make the mushrooms release some of their moisture, helping them to brown. Depending on what kind of mushrooms you're using, 5 to 10 minutes should be enough. Set aside.

To grill, your coals should be so hot that you can comfortably keep your hand 2 inches above the grate for 3 seconds—just! (For gas grills, this means 450°F.) Put the oiled steak on the hottest part of the grill and sear for 3 to 5 minutes on each side. Most flank steak won't need more cooking than that; if it needs more cooking, move to lower heat for at most 2 to 5 minutes more—it should always be rare! **To pan-fry,** heat the peanut oil in a heavy pan until it's very hot—almost smoking. Sear the steaks for 3 minutes on each side over high heat before turning down the burner. Cook for at most 2 to 5 minutes more over moderate heat, turning the steak often. Again, it doesn't take much time to cook a flank steak, and a good sear will mean the steak is cooked more than enough.

However you cook your steak, check for doneness often, using the finger-poke or the nick-and-peek method (see page 19). Generously salt and pepper the meat before resting it in the warming oven (170°F) or on a warm plate under a loose tent of foil for 5 minutes.

Remove the steak from the oven and slice against the grain (that means across, cutting short rather than long slices). Portion out the steak in the center of warm plates, top with the mushrooms, followed by some potatoes to surround the steak. The plate should have a happily disheveled look. Give the food a final pinch of Maldon salt, a generous grind of black pepper, and you're done.

Robinson Bar Potatoes

Named after the nineteenth-century guest ranch in rural Idaho that my family bought in 1976, this dish is my father's invention. Idaho in winter is a cold, dark place. In January, it wasn't uncommon for the thermometer to stay below zero for a week. These potatoes, I imagine, were invented on a January night—they're gonzo comfort food. What distinguishes them from other scalloped potatoes are the thin layers, the Comté cheese, and the touch of nutmeg.

The trick to getting the recipe right is to use the right kind of cheese and not too much cream. I feel pretty strongly about the virtues of Comté, a French mountain cheese with a strong bite and nuttiness to it. Gruyère or Emmental are good substitutes.

6 medium red potatoes

1 clove garlic

2 to 3 tablespoons unsalted butter

Kosher salt and freshly ground black pepper

1/2 cup grated Comté cheese

1/3 cup heavy cream

Whole nutmeg

Preheat the oven to 400°F.

You don't have to peel the potatoes for this dish, but I usually do. Either way, cut the potatoes into thin slices (1/8-inch thick)—a mandoline makes this easy. Drop the slices into cold water as you go.

Slice the garlic diagonally and rub it around a dry, shallow baking dish. (You may need just one dish, if you have a large one, or two smaller ones. The potatoes should be layered 3 deep. Period. Use your ingredients as your guide.) Generously butter the dish. Dry the potatoes on a towel and layer them in the bottom of the pan so they *just* overlap. Sprinkle salt and pepper on that layer and add one-third of the grated cheese. Repeat this process with the next two layers of potatoes. Finally, add the cream. Stop when it *almost* reaches the top layer of potatoes—you don't want that top layer to be floating. Dot the top with butter and shave on just a hint of fresh nutmeg (less than 1/4 teaspoon).

Bake for 30 minutes or so. The potatoes are done when the top is nicely browned and most of the cream has been absorbed by the potatoes.

Strip Steak with Green Peppercorn Sauce,
Crispy Fried Shallots, and Fennel Gratin

This is an elemental meal—there's something about the flavors that is refreshingly unfussy—like good pub food. If you don't have any chicken juices, use twice the chicken stock called for here, for a total of 1¹/₃ cups.

Serves 4

GRILL OR PAN-FRY

4 strip steaks

1 teaspoon kosher salt

Olive oil for rubbing

1 to 2 tablespoons peanut oil for pan-frying

Freshly ground black pepper

GREEN PEPPERCORN SAUCE

¹/₄ cup chicken juices (see page 22)

2 tablespoons dried green peppercorns, coarsely ground

2 tablespoons your best vinegar

²/₃ cup chicken stock (page 26)

¹/₂ cup heavy cream

Kosher salt

Prepare the steaks by salting them, and then let them come to room temperature. Rub them with olive oil just before cooking.

To grill, your coals should be so hot that you can comfortably keep your hand 2 inches above the grate for 3 seconds—just! (For gas grills, this means 450°F.) Put the oiled steaks on the hottest part of the grill and sear for 3 to 5 minutes on each side over intense heat before you begin to fuss over them. That means moving the steaks to a cooler part of the grill and cooking more gently for an additional 6 to 10 minutes over moderate heat, flipping, poking, and watching as you work toward crispy-brown perfection. **To pan-fry,** heat the peanut oil in a heavy pan until it's very hot—almost smoking. Sear the steaks for 3 minutes on each side over high heat before turning down the burner. Cook over moderate heat for an additional 6 to 10 minutes, turning the steaks every few minutes as they slowly brown. Rather than burning the pan, which you will use to make your sauce, finish cooking thicker steaks by putting them, pan and all, in a 400°F oven.

However you cook your steaks, check for doneness often, using the finger-poke method, an instant-read thermometer (120° to 130°F for rare to medium-rare), or the nick-and-peek method (see page 19). Generously salt and pepper each steak before resting them in the warming oven (170°F) or on a warm plate under a loose tent of foil for 5 minutes.

Combine the chicken juices, green peppercorns, and vinegar in the pan you cooked the steak in (if you grilled, just start a fresh pan). Heat the mixture until it begins to simmer, and then add the chicken stock. Return to a simmer before whisking in the cream. Reduce by half (3 to 6 minutes), or until the sauce thickens and yields a little more than half a cup. Taste the sauce, adding kosher salt as needed.

After the steaks have rested, pour a little pool of the sauce onto each plate, put the steak on top of it, and the Crispy Fried Shallots on top of that. Add some of the Fennel Gratin and your dinner is ready to eat.

Crispy Fried Shallots

The size of shallots varies. Look for large ones and be sure they're fresh (no soft spots, sprouts, or black centers).

5 large shallots, peeled and thinly sliced

1 cup flour

2 tablespoons unsalted butter

Kosher salt

Toss the shallot slices in the flour, pushing the layers apart so they look like doll-size onion rings. When they're coated, shake them over the sink in a small wire colander to get rid of the excess flour.

Heat the butter in a large frying pan over low heat. Add the shallots in a single layer and cook them without browning the butter. Flip the slices gently after about 5 minutes. They should be starting to color, which means they're almost done. Since they'll continue to cook once you take them out of the pan, leave them for just another 2 minutes on side two, removing them before they darken too much. Transfer to a wire rack or paper towel, sprinkle with kosher salt, and, if your steaks aren't ready yet, place in a warming oven (170°F). These little guys are best hot and fresh.

Fennel Gratin

1 tablespoon butter

1 shallot, peeled and sliced

3 fennel bulbs, outer layer removed, thinly sliced (reserve the tops)

2/3 cup light cream

2/3 cup grated Cheddar cheese

1 teaspoon kosher salt

Freshly ground black pepper

Preheat the oven to 350°F. Smear a shallow baking dish (around 8 by 11 inches) with butter and then lay the shallot slices in a single layer, followed by a layer of the sliced fennel. Pour in the cream and sprinkle on the grated cheese and the salt. Cover loosely with foil and bake for 20 minutes. Remove the foil and bake for an additional 5 to 10 minutes. The top layer should be beginning to brown and the liquid should be reduced. Remove the gratin from the oven and let it stand for 5 minutes to set. To serve, tear or chop several pieces of the reserved fennel tops and sprinkle them on top, along with a generous grind of fresh black pepper.

Flat Iron Steak with Roquefort Butter
and Coriander Brussels Sprouts

Simple, fast, and bracing, this is a good meal for a Monday night, when you need something to fortify yourself for the week ahead. The Roquefort butter should be just a melted smear of flavor on your steak—not a big glob on the side. You shouldn't see the butter; you should taste it. Coriander Brussels Sprouts make it a meal. Fingerling Potatoes (page 138) would make a great addition, too.

Making blue cheese butter is an excuse to explore a few of the great blues American producers are making from Point Reyes, California, to the Finger Lakes in New York. If you prefer to stick to the European classics, Fourme d'Ambert is my favorite French blue. It's both creamy and powerful. Standard French Roquefort is also good, if saltier, while the Italian Gorgonzola can be a bit strong to my taste. British-made Stilton is always a good option, while the better Danish blues are safely soft, creamy, and mild.

Serves 4

GRILL OR PAN-FRY

4 flat iron steaks (about 2 pounds)

1 teaspoon kosher salt

Olive oil for rubbing

1 to 2 tablespoons peanut oil for pan-frying

ROQUEFORT BUTTER

1/4 cup (about 2 ounces) Roquefort

4 tablespoons unsalted butter, softened

Prepare the steaks by removing the line of gristle that runs down the center. I usually cut the steak into 2 rectangular pieces. As you cut, try to work around the concentration of white gristle at the center of the steak. Salt the steaks, and then let them come to room temperature. Rub them with olive oil just before cooking.

To make the butter, blend the cheese and the butter with a fork, integrating them thoroughly. Set aside on the counter.

To grill, your coals should be so hot that you can comfortably keep your hand 2 inches above the grate for 3 seconds—just! (For gas grills, this means 450°F.) Put the oiled steaks on the hottest part of the grill and sear for 3 to 5 minutes on each side over high heat before you begin to fuss over them. That means moving the steaks to a cooler part of the grill and cooking for 6 to 10 minutes, flipping, poking, and watching as you work toward crispy-brown perfection. **To pan-fry,** heat the peanut oil in a heavy pan until it's very hot—almost smoking. Sear the steaks for 3 minutes on each side over high heat before turning down the burner. Cook for an additional 6 to 10 minutes over moderate heat, turning the steaks every few minutes as they slowly brown. Finish cooking thicker steaks by putting them, pan and all, in a 400°F oven.

However you cook your steaks, check for doneness often, using the finger-poke method, an instant-read thermometer

(120° to 130°F for rare to medium-rare), or the nick-and-peek method (see page 19).

After cooking, smear on that butter—using it all—before resting the steaks in the warming oven (170°F) for 5 minutes. The butter should melt while the meat is in the oven.

Once the steaks are done resting, put them on warm plates, pouring some of the buttery meat juices over each steak. Pile some of the Brussels sprouts on each plate.

Coriander Brussels Sprouts

2 pounds Brussels sprouts

1 tablespoon whole coriander

3 tablespoons unsalted butter

1 cup chicken stock

1 teaspoon kosher salt

Trim the stem end of the Brussels sprouts and peel away any rough or discolored outer leaves. Cut each bulb in half; cut very large ones into quarters. Using a mortar and pestle or a spice grinder, crush the coriander just until no whole seeds remain. Heat 2 tablespoons of the butter in a large frying pan and add the Brussels sprouts. Stir to coat with the butter, then add the stock and salt. Cover the pan and cook over medium heat. After 5 minutes, remove the lid from the pan, add the coriander and the remaining 1 tablespoon of butter, and turn the heat to high. You want to eliminate any remaining moisture in the pan while browning the butter. The pan should get hot! Taste for tenderness and seasoning—add salt as needed. When they're ready to serve, the Brussels sprouts should be tender but still firm. Transfer to a bowl and serve.

Sherry-Chanterelle Sauce over Hangar Steak
with Golden Beets and Braised Endive

Here's the most old-world sauce in the book. Chanterelles can be hard to find. Markets like Whole Foods have made the quest more attainable for many— but not for all. If you just can't get your hands on any, and there aren't other varieties of wild mushrooms around, use dried morels. They retain their flavor better when dried than does the delicate chanterelle. I like this steak with the simple sweetness of Golden Beets alongside Braised Endive, which nicely cuts the richness of the creamy sauce. If you don't have any chicken juices, use a total of 3/4 cup chicken stock.

Serves 4
GRILL OR PAN-FRY

1 hangar steak (about 2 pounds)

1 teaspoon kosher salt

Olive oil for rubbing

2 tablespoons peanut oil for pan-frying

Freshly ground black pepper

SHERRY-CHANTERELLE SAUCE

3/4 pound chanterelle mushrooms or 2 to 3 ounces dried mushrooms

4 tablespoons unsalted butter

1 shallot, minced (1 tablespoon)

3 tablespoons chicken juices (see page 22) or 1/2 cup chicken stock (page 26)

1/4 cup chicken stock

1 tablespoon dry sherry (not cooking sherry from the grocery store!)

1/2 cup heavy cream

1/4 teaspoon kosher salt

Freshly ground black pepper

Prepare the hangar steak by removing the tendon that runs down its center (see page 56). If your steak is looking a bit ravaged, you can use kitchen twine to tie the two pieces back together. Simply set the steak on the counter in the shape it was before you cut it up and criss-cross the string over and under it, finishing with a knot. Salt the steak, and then let it come to room temperature. Rub with olive oil just before cooking.

To make the sauce, prepare the mushrooms. Fresh mushrooms are dry to the touch, never slimy. Discard or trim any that have gone bad. Then trim the ends and brush off any stray dirt or pine needles. By all means, don't wash them. Slice the large mushrooms in half, leaving the smaller ones whole.

In a heavy frying pan, gently heat 1 tablespoon of the butter and the shallot. Cook for 1 to 2 minutes until just soft. Add the chicken juices and blend with a wire whisk. Add the stock, sherry, and cream. Cook over medium-low heat for 6 to 12 minutes to reduce by half. The sauce should be thick— the consistency of very rich heavy cream. Turn off the heat and set aside.

To grill, your coals should be so hot that you can comfortably keep your hand 2 inches above the grate for 3 seconds— just! (For gas grills, this means 450°F.) Put the oiled steak on the hottest part of the grill and sear for 3 to 5 minutes on each side over high heat before you begin to fuss over it. That means moving the steak to a cooler part of the grill and cooking for an additional 10 to 14 minutes over moderate heat, flipping, poking, and watching as you work toward crispy-brown perfection. **To pan-fry,** heat the peanut oil in a heavy pan until it's very hot—almost smoking. Sear the steak for 3 minutes on each side over high heat before lowering the burner.

Cook over moderate heat for an additional 10 to 14 minutes, turning the steak every few minutes as it slowly browns. Rather than setting off the smoke alarm, you can finish cooking the steak by putting it, pan and all, in a 400°F oven.

However you cook the steak, check for doneness often, using the finger-poke method, an instant-read thermometer (120° to 130°F for rare to medium-rare), or the nick-and-peek method (see page 19). Generously salt and pepper each steak before resting it in the warming oven (170°F) or on a warm plate under a loose tent of foil for 5 minutes.

While the steaks cook, put the mushrooms and the remaining 3 tablespoons of butter in a separate frying pan over medium-high heat. Cook for 5 minutes while they absorb the butter. Keep them moving in the pan. When the pan is dry and hot, add the salt. Continue to cook for another minute or two as the mushrooms release their moisture. They should be faintly browned on the edges and firm but not spongy when you bite down. Transfer most of the mushrooms to a plate and into a warming oven (170°F), reserving one-third.

To finish the sauce, coarsely chop the reserved mushrooms. Add them to the sauce along with a grind of fresh black pepper. Reheat, whisk, and taste. The sauce should be rich, thick, and highly seasoned. Add more salt to taste. If the sauce is too thick or at all gummy, add a little stock or cream.

Place the steaks in the center of your plates and then pour the sauce over. Sprinkle the remaining mushrooms on top. Your Golden Beets and Braised Endive should be ready; arrange them around the steak, alternating endive and beets to give the plate color.

Golden Beets

Leaving the skin on the beets makes them prettier and tastier.

3 beets, skins on

2 tablespoons extra virgin olive oil

1/2 teaspoon kosher salt

Freshly ground black pepper

Preheat the oven to 375°F. Scrub the beets and cut off the ends, then quarter them. Lay out one large sheet of aluminum foil and another of equal length across it to form a cross. Place the beets in the center, where the foil is doubled, and drizzle on the olive oil. Run the beets around on the foil to coat them on all sides with the oil before wrapping them up like a present and sticking them in the oven for an hour. Depending on the size of the beets you're using, an hour will be plenty; for very small beets, check for doneness after 45 minutes. They should be tender but still firm.

Put the cooked beets in a bowl, pouring any juices or oil remaining in the foil over the beets. Add the salt and pepper and serve.

Braised Endive

2 heads endive, quartered

1 tablespoon olive oil

1 teaspoon kosher salt

Freshly ground black pepper

Preheat the oven to 375°F. Tuck the endive quarters into a small, shallow baking dish. Add the oil and move the pieces around to coat. The endive should fit in the dish fairly snugly, so each piece is touching. Sprinkle on the salt and cover with foil. Bake for 20 to 25 minutes. Add freshly ground pepper before serving.

Bolognese Sauce
over Homemade Noodles with Garlic Bread

This is a job for a long winter afternoon—it requires some time and attention. But it's an excuse to putter around the kitchen, and you will like the reward. What's this sauce doing in a steak book? While there are many versions of the classic Bolognese sauce out there, almost all of them are made with some combination of ground beef, veal, and pork. This one is different, and it's in this book because it calls for skirt steak. I have Alice Waters's classic *Chez Panisse Café Cookbook* to thank for inspiring me to use skirt steak this way. I've never been a fan of ground beef in sauces, but here the meaty bites of tender, slow-cooked steak are a revelation, giving the sauce a nice texture and richness. I've added sweet basil, and, where Alice's recipe uses only tomato paste, I call for the addition of some crushed Italian tomatoes toward the end of the process, along with a bit of lemon peel. You can't go wrong drinking any red wine with this meal. But this is also a good excuse to open that expensive bottle of wine you've been saving. Don't forget the Homemade Noodles and Garlic Bread.

Serves 4

LONG, SLOW COOK ON
THE STOVE

1/2 cup dried porcini mushrooms, soaked and chopped (use 1 cup chopped fresh porcini if you can, of course)

3 to 5 tablespoons olive oil

1 1/2 pounds skirt steak, cut into 1/4-inch cubes (or substitute top blade steak, which is both fatty and flavorful)

1/4 pound ground pork (chopped pork loin works in a pinch)

1/4 pound pancetta, diced

1 yellow onion, diced

5 ribs celery, diced

1 carrot, diced

1/4 teaspoon salt

4 cloves garlic, finely chopped

1 cup dry white wine (a pinot grigio is a fine choice)

4 sprigs of fresh thyme

This isn't a difficult recipe, but there are many small steps as you add ingredients, allowing your sauce to slowly build its complex flavor as it reduces. Begin by pouring boiling water over the porcini mushrooms, just covering them. Let them sit for 15 minutes.

Meanwhile, put 2 tablespoons of the olive oil into a large, heavy, fairly deep sauté pan. You'll be using this pan from start to finish. When the oil is hot, add about one-third of your cut-up meat. You're caramelizing the meat, not cooking it, so it's imperative to work in small batches. (If you toss it all in the pan at once, it will steam rather than brown.) Working in 3 batches, brown the meat all over, setting the cooked pieces aside as you go. Cooking takes about 5 minutes per batch, turning occasionally, since the pieces are small. You want a brown crust on the outside and that pleasant smell of sizzling meat. Again, no need to cook it through. Once you're finished, remove the meat, add the pork to the pan, and brown it for a minute in the hot oil. Remove from the pan and set the pork aside.

Get your pancetta going over medium-high heat in your trusty pan (gently scrape it with a wooden spoon to loosen any bits of meat; if it's dry, add 2 tablespoons of olive oil). Once the pancetta begins to brown a little (after about 5 minutes), add the chopped onion, celery, and carrots and mix. Salt

2 bay leaves

2 cups chicken stock (page 26)

1 1/2 cups whole milk

3 tablespoons Italian tomato paste

1 cup canned Italian plum tomatoes, chopped

Zest from 1/2 lemon, organic if possible

Freshly ground black pepper

5 leaves basil, chopped

4 sprigs of Italian parsley, chopped, for garnish

Parmigiano-Reggiano

lightly, allowing the mixture to cook for 5 minutes, or until the carrots begin to caramelize, then add the porcini (drain them first) and the garlic. Cook a few minutes more.

Now, turning the heat down to medium-low, return the pork and steak to the pan and add the wine, thyme sprigs, and bay leaves. Allow the mixture to reduce, stirring and scraping the pan as it cooks. Once it's really beginning to stick to the pan (don't let it) and the mix is browning, add 1 cup of the stock, 1/4 cup of the milk, and the tomato paste. Allow the new liquid to reduce the same way, occasionally scraping the bottom of the pan to prevent burning. Skim any visible fat off the surface as you work. Allow the sauce to simmer slowly, adding the remaining 1 cup of stock and the remaining 1 1/4 cups of milk in a couple of small batches, reducing it all between each addition. The sauce should cook for about 1 1/2 hours for the meat to become tender. Turn down the heat if it's reducing too quickly.

About 10 minutes before the sauce is done, add the plum tomatoes, lemon zest, freshly ground pepper, and chopped basil. Cook off most of the liquid. The sauce should be fairly solid, not soupy. Taste for salt before serving. I find the sauce doesn't need salt, but be your own judge. Remember, the cheese you'll add at the end is quite salty, too.

Serve in warm pasta bowls over Homemade Noodles with a sprinkle of parsley and grated cheese. I like this with Garlic Bread and a big, solid Italian Barbaresco.

Homemade Noodles

The quality and freshness of your eggs *and* your flour will make a big difference in how these noodles taste. Also, if you don't have one, this is the time to buy a combination pasta roller and cutter (they aren't expensive). These machines make homemade noodles simple. I wouldn't try to make them without one.

3 cups unbleached, all-purpose flour

1 teaspoon kosher salt

3 eggs

About 1/2 cup cool water

Semolina flour

Olive oil

In a large bowl, combine the flour and salt. Make a well in the center of the flour. You're clearing a circle for the eggs, which you should dump there now. Using your fingers, gently and slowly incorporate the surrounding flour with the eggs. You shouldn't work the dough—just try to mix the flour and eggs. You'll almost certainly need some water to finish the job—it depends on how big your eggs are and how dry your flour is. (Flour varies widely in how much moisture it contains.)

Make a ball of dough that's neither too sticky nor impossible to hold together. It's easy to add too much water and end up with very sticky dough. Take the process slowly and really work the dough through before you add more water.

Once you have a ball that neither sticks to your hands nor falls apart, put it on a clean surface and begin to work it with a very light dusting of flour. From this point on, you shouldn't need much extra flour. Knead the dough vigorously, pushing and folding it back over onto itself repeatedly, for a full 15 minutes. What began as a lumpy mass will become a smooth, integrated, and very pliable whole. I love this part of the process—it's oddly satisfying and peaceful even if it is a little tiring. Take your time, feel the dough, and enjoy the work. When the time's up, your arms will be ready for a break.

Cover the dough with plastic wrap and let it rest for an hour at room temperature.

There are two steps involved in preparing the noodles: rolling and cutting.

To roll the noodles, slice off a hunk of the dough and use your hands to shape it into a rectangle that is thin enough to feed into the pasta machine. Adjust the roller to its thickest setting. You're going to run the dough through at least twice, once on that thick setting and again on a thinner setting. Keep in mind that noodles that are too thick can be gummy. (If you want thick noodles, make them a few hours ahead and let them dry out a bit before cooking them.) If the dough tears, simply fold it over on itself and feed it back through the roller again.

Second, cut the rolled dough into noodles: flour each piece lightly to prevent the cut noodles from sticking together. Set the cutter to the size noodle you want. Fettuccine is easy to handle and appealing on the plate. Feed the dough through the cutter, catching it as it comes out, like magic, on the other side. At this stage, it's helpful to have another set of hands— my eight-year-old daughter likes to help me by turning the crank while I feed the dough through. Lay the noodles gently on a clean cookie sheet that's been dusted with a little semolina flour.

Cover the noodles with plastic wrap to prevent them from drying out. If you'll be using them within an hour or so, let them sit out on the counter. If it's going to be longer than that, put the cookie sheet in the refrigerator to keep the noodles moist.

Cook the pasta in as much boiling, lightly salted water as you can fit in your biggest pot; add a generous splash of olive oil to prevent sticking. These noodles cook very quickly, depending on their thickness. Test fettuccine after 2 minutes and take them out when they taste *almost* done. They will continue to cook once drained. After draining, prevent the noodles from sticking together by putting them back into the pot and tossing them gently with a tablespoon of olive oil and a little kosher salt.

Garlic Bread

Using great bread and olive oil is the key to making delicious garlic bread—make plenty.

3 cloves garlic, peeled

3 tablespoons good olive oil

6 to 8 slices great bread or
1 long (24-inch) baguette, split lengthwise

1 teaspoon kosher salt

This is one of the few times I use a garlic press. You can use yours, too. Just press the garlic through into a small bowl and stir it around with the olive oil. Let it sit for 5 minutes before you drizzle it on the bread as evenly as you can. If you're working with slices, stack them to coat both sides. Sprinkle the bread with salt and, if you've split a baguette, close it up until you're ready to toast it.

Cook the bread under a broiler. Watch it *very* carefully—bread burns in a flash under a direct flame. When it's done, each slice should be a toasty brown with no black spots. You can also grill the bread either in your fireplace using a Tuscan Grill (see the Pantry section at the end of the book) or on a regular grill.

Rib Steak with Anchovy Butter,
Three-Root Mashers, and Garlic–Cherry Tomato Reduction

Anchovy butter is a fine thing—it matches up with a steak like little else. Call it the umami factor. The Garlic–Cherry Tomato Reduction brightens everything up, while the Three-Root Mashers complete the meal.

Serves 4

GRILL OR PAN-FRY

4 rib steaks, bone-in or boneless

1 teaspoon kosher salt

Olive oil for rubbing

1 to 2 tablespoons peanut oil for pan-frying

Freshly ground pepper

ANCHOVY BUTTER

8 anchovy filets

4 tablespoons unsalted butter, at room temperature

Pinch of cayenne pepper

2 tablespoons chopped flat-leaf parsley, for garnish

Prepare the steaks by salting them, and then let them come to room temperature. Rub with olive oil just before cooking.

To make the butter, mince the anchovies until they're basically fish pulp. Thoroughly mix the anchovies with the butter and cayenne. Set aside.

To grill, your coals should be so hot that you can comfortably keep your hand 2 inches above the grate for 3 seconds—just! (For gas grills, this means 450°F.) Put the oiled steaks on the hottest part of the grill and sear for 3 to 5 minutes on each side before you begin to fuss over them. That means moving the steaks to a cooler part of the grill and cooking for an additional 8 to 12 minutes over moderate heat, flipping, poking, and watching as you work toward crispy-brown perfection. **To pan-fry,** heat the peanut oil in a heavy pan until it's very hot—almost smoking. Sear the steaks for 3 minutes on each side over high heat before lowering the burner. Cook for an additional 8 to 12 minutes over moderate heat, turning the steaks every few minutes as they slowly brown. Finish cooking thicker steaks by putting them, pan and all, in a 400°F oven.

However you cook your steaks, check for doneness often, using the finger-poke method, an instant-read thermometer (120° to 130°F for rare to medium-rare), or the nick-and-peek method (see page 19). Generously pepper each steak (don't salt them—the Anchovy Butter is quite salty) before resting them in the warming oven (170°F) or on a warm plate under a loose tent of foil for 5 minutes.

To serve, spread the Anchovy Butter over the surface of the hot steaks and place them on the plates with some of the mashers. Finish by scattering parsley over both the steak and the tomato.

Three-Root Mashers

With the added edge of the turnip and parsnip, these have a more grown-up flavor than plain mashed potatoes.

3 small parsnips, peeled and ends trimmed

1 small turnip (^{1}/$_2$ pound), peeled

5 medium Yukon Gold potatoes (1^1/$_2$ pounds), washed with skin on

^{1}/$_2$ cup heavy cream

^{1}/$_2$ cup whole milk

2 tablespoons butter

1^1/$_2$ teaspoons salt

Freshly ground black pepper

Cut the parsnips, turnips, and potatoes into similar-size chunks. Put them in a pot with a lid and a steamer basket set over boiling water and cook, covered, for 20 to 30 minutes at medium heat. When a fork meets no resistance when it's stuck into the center of the largest piece, pour the cooked vegetables into a colander to drain. (Test the parsnips separately if they are much smaller and remove them before the other vegetables if necessary.)

Using the same pot the vegetables steamed in (but without the vegetables), scald the cream and milk by heating it not quite to a boil. Add the drained vegetables to the scalded milk-cream mixture, along with the butter, salt, and pepper to taste. Now gently mash it all together. Don't overwork or try to get it too smooth. A few lumps, along with the skins, provide texture and pleasure. Eat.

Garlic–Cherry Tomato Reduction

This is how I take my tomatoes in January or anytime when I get a craving for this bright little fruit but there aren't any good ones to be found. If you have really dreary tomatoes, you could add a splash of good balsamic vinegar.

3 cups cherry tomatoes

3 tablespoons chopped garlic

2 tablespoons olive oil

^{1}/$_2$ teaspoon kosher salt

Cut the tomatoes in half and put them in a large sauté pan with the garlic, olive oil, and salt. Cook over medium-high heat, stirring occasionally, for 15 to 20 minutes. The tomatoes will get very soupy and watery about midway through the process; don't worry, they'll move through this stage and begin to thicken and even start to stick to the bottom of the pan. When this happens, they're done. Taste for salt and serve.

Steak au Poivre,
French Fries, and Endive Salad

This classic steak evokes the red booths, long white aprons, and diffused yellow light that makes everyone in a bustling French bistro—not just the models and French waiters—look good. This is a steak that calls for potatoes, a simple salad, and a lot of red wine. Don't be put off by the idea of making the meat reduction. It's not at all hard and can be done ahead. Serve with French Fries and Endive Salad.

Serves 4

GRILL OR PAN-FRY

2 pounds hangar steak

1 teaspoon kosher salt

Olive oil for rubbing

4 tablespoons whole black peppercorns, coarsely ground (use a mortar and pestle or a spice grinder)

1 to 2 tablespoons peanut oil for pan-frying

Freshly ground black pepper

PEPPER SAUCE

3 oxtails or other inexpensive meat (6 ounces or so)

1 tablespoon peanut oil

2 shallots, finely chopped (3 tablespoons)

$1/2$ cup chicken juices (see page 22) or 1 cup chicken stock (page 26)

$1/2$ cup cognac or good brandy, plus a splash

1 cup heavy cream

1 tablespoon unsalted butter

Kosher salt

I've never seen hangar steak in the supermarket; you'll probably have to make a trip to a butcher or order it and have it shipped to you. Ask them to cut out the tendon that runs down the center of the steak, or do it yourself (see page 56 for instructions).

Salt the steak generously, rub it with oil, and press the ground pepper into both sides. I like to grind my pepper using a mortar and pestle, which leaves each berry cracked, but not pulverized. In any case, you want a balance between finely and coarsely ground. Cover the meat and set it aside to come to room temperature.

To make the sauce, any inexpensive cut of meat will work. If you're using oxtails, before frying the bones, cut off any of the meat you can. Cook the scraps and bones in the peanut oil in a good-size sauté pan over medium-high heat. Turn and scrape often. After 5 minutes, when everything is browned and a bit of the fat has rendered off, remove the bones and any meat, leaving no more than 2 to 3 tablespoons of fat in the pan along with the flavorful bits (reserve the bones). Return the pan to the heat and add the shallots, cooking over medium heat until they're soft, about 5 minutes.

Now, add the chicken juices and $1/2$ cup of cognac. If you're cooking on a gas stove, watch out for flare-ups! Cook to reduce by half, 6 to 12 minutes (reduce longer if you're using stock instead of chicken juices). I also like to return the bones to the pan at this point, letting them simmer to give up more of their flavor. Skim off any scum that forms. When the liquid has reduced, remove the bones, add the cream, and reduce again by half, 3 to 6 minutes. At this point, the nearly finished sauce can be set aside until you're ready to use it.

To grill, your coals should be so hot that you can comfortably keep your hand 2 inches above the grate for 3 seconds— just! (For gas grills, this means 450°F.) Put the oiled steak on the hottest part of the grill and sear for 3 to 5 minutes on each side before you begin to fuss over it. That means moving the steak to a cooler part of the grill and cooking for an additional 10 to 14 minutes over more moderate heat, flipping, poking, and watching as you work toward crispy-brown perfection.

To pan-fry, heat the peanut oil in a heavy pan until it's very hot—almost smoking. Sear the steak for 3 minutes on each side over high heat before turning down the burner. Cook over moderate heat for an additional 10 to 14 minutes, turning the steak every few minutes as it slowly browns—but be careful not to burn the pepper.

Hangar steak is thin in some places, thick in others. This makes it a little tricky to cook, although it often means there are some very rare pieces right alongside the more cooked ones. However you cook your steak, check for doneness often, using the finger-poke method, an instant-read thermometer (120° to 130°F for rare to medium-rare), or the nick-and-peek method (see page 19). Generously salt and pepper the steak before resting it in the warming oven (170°F) or on a warm plate under a loose tent of foil for 5 minutes.

While the meat rests, finish your sauce by adding a splash of cognac and the butter, whisking as you reheat it. When it's hot, it's ready. Taste and add salt as needed. Slice the steak into 1-inch-thick medalions, and place on warm plates. Spoon some sauce over each one. Pile up a tower of fries on one side of the plate and put the salad opposite.

French Fries

I hate making French fries without a deep fryer. Can it be done? Sure, just heat up a big pot of oil and spatter away. But it's messy and borders on dangerous. It's also not easy to get the oil to the right temperature and keep it there.

4 large russet potatoes, peeled (4 to 5 pounds)

Peanut oil or half peanut, half vegetable oil for frying (3 to 4 inches in a pot; about 1 gallon for most home fryers)

Kosher salt

Ideally, you will peel your potatoes the night before you want to make these fries and let them soak in water overnight. In the morning, change the water and let them soak some more before using a mandoline to cut them. If you're not that organized, just peel the potatoes and drop them into a bowl of cold water. Drain the water after you've peeled them all but before you begin cutting the fries. The idea is to get as much of the starch out as possible.

The more uniform your fries, the more evenly they will cook. This is what a mandoline does, so if you're using one, great—run those potatoes through. If not, do what you can to keep the slices about the same size. I usually cut each potato into slices the long way, pull the potato in half, and then lay each half flat on the counter to cut it into lengths. As you work, drop the cut fries into cold water and let them soak, changing the water frequently.

You will be cooking your fries twice. To do this, heat your oil to 320°F for round one. Cook in manageable batches for 5 to 6 minutes. You will not be browning them at this stage. As they come out, place them on a wire rack set over a cookie sheet or on paper towels to drain. Let the half-cooked fries cool for 10 minutes or for as long as several hours before you fry them the second time.

For the second round, heat the oil to 375°F. This time, leave them in until they turn a nice caramel brown—between 2 and 3 minutes. Remove to a rack or to paper towels and salt liberally. Taste one. A pillowy soft center and a crispy, salty exterior is what you're after. Serve immediately.

Endive Salad

2 to 3 heads endive, depending on size (2 cups chopped)

2 tablespoons your best olive oil

1 tablespoon lemon juice (Meyer if you can get it)

$1/4$ teaspoon kosher salt

Freshly ground black pepper

The creamy-yellow and white endive should be firm, not limp. Peel back and discard any discolored outer leaves and chop off the stem end. From the stem up, keep slicing across, creating $1/2$-inch-thick pieces shaped like half rounds of cut celery. Toss in a bowl with the olive oil, lemon juice, salt, and pepper. Taste and adjust the seasoning as needed.

Steak Florentine,
Herb Polenta, and Stuffed Squash Blossoms

Traditionally, *Bistecca a la Fiorentina* is a simply cooked dry-aged porterhouse or T-bone from the Chianina, the classic white cow of Tuscany. It might be served plain or accompanied by chopped herbs, a little balsamic vinegar, and olive oil. Long employed in the Italian countryside for plowing and farm labor, these cows are now bred in the United States. Chianina steaks are hard to come by, but big dry-aged steaks cooked on the grill will work, too. The Herb Polenta and Stuffed Squash Blossoms will complete the plate nicely. An Italian red to drink and some fresh mozzarella served with basil and summer tomatoes would make a great starter.

Serves 4

GRILL OR PAN-FRY

4 T-bone steaks, preferably dry aged

1 teaspoon kosher salt

Olive oil for rubbing

1 to 2 tablespoons peanut oil for pan-frying

Freshly ground black pepper

1 clove garlic, peeled and lightly crushed

4 teaspoons balsamic vinegar (the best you can afford)

Good olive oil for drizzling

Parmigiano-Reggiano for garnish

1 tablespoon chopped oregano

1 tablespoon chopped sage

1 tablespoon chopped parsley

Prepare the steaks by salting them, and then let them come to room temperature. Rub the steak with olive oil just before cooking.

To grill, your coals should be so hot that you can comfortably keep your hand 2 inches above the grate for 3 seconds—just! (For gas grills, this means 450°F.) Put the oiled steaks on the hottest part of the grill and sear for 3 to 5 minutes on each side over high heat before you begin to fuss over them. That means moving the steaks to a cooler part of the grill and cooking for an additional 8 to 12 minutes over moderate heat, flipping, poking, and watching as you work toward crispy-brown perfection. **To pan-fry,** heat the peanut oil in a heavy pan until it's very hot—almost smoking. Sear the steaks for 3 minutes on each side over high heat before turning down the burner. Cook over moderate heat for an additional 8 to 12 minutes, turning every few minutes as they slowly brown. Finish cooking thicker steaks by putting them, pan and all, in a 400°F oven.

However you cook your steaks, check for doneness often, using the finger-poke method, an instant-read thermometer (120° to 130°F for rare to medium-rare), or the nick-and-peek method (see page 19). Generously salt and pepper each steak and rub it with the garlic clove before resting them in the warming oven (170°F) or on a warm plate under a loose tent of foil for 5 minutes.

Once the steaks have rested, put them on warm plates and spoon 1 teaspoon of balsamic vinegar in a thin line down each one followed by just a few drops of fruity, green olive oil. Portion out the polenta and stuffed blossoms before scattering the herbs and a fine grating of Parmigiano-Reggiano over everything. For the full experience—short of a plane ticket—drink a bottle of Barolo with this meal.

Herb Polenta

5 cups water

2 teaspoons kosher salt

1 cup medium-grain polenta

2 tablespoons unsalted butter

Your best olive oil

3 tablespoons chopped herbs (use any combination of thyme, basil, parsley, oregano, and chives)

Bring the water to a boil in a medium saucepan. Add the salt and then slowly add the polenta, whisking to combine. Simmer over low heat, stirring frequently. The polenta will slowly thicken and after 15 minutes or so you may need to add some water. Try adding $^1/_2$ cup. Cook for at least 30 minutes; longer is better. If you continue to add water, a little at a time, you can cook polenta for almost an hour. When you take the polenta off the heat it should be thick, with the bubbles that rise up through the porridge struggling to come through and popping as they erupt.

Add the butter and stir until it's completely melted. Let it set for 5 minutes before serving. When you're ready to eat, pour the polenta into a serving bowl or onto individual plates with the steak. Before serving, drizzle on a little of your best olive oil and scatter the herbs on top.

Stuffed Squash Blossoms

I love edible flowers, especially squash blossoms. When they're stuffed with seasoned ricotta, they become a delicious summer obsession. For cooks with gardens, getting the blossoms is easy—by mid-July they're popping up from squash and pumpkin plants in every direction. For nongardeners, farmers' markets are a good place to look. The blossoms with a tiny squash or zucchini attached are the ones I most prize. To make this dish, you'll need a pastry tube, but no tip is required. Alternatively, use a plastic bag with a hole cut in the corner.

2 cups sheep's milk ricotta (cow's milk ricotta works too, if it's fresh)

1/4 cup chopped basil, chives, and thyme

2 tablespoons olive oil

1 teaspoon kosher salt

1/3 cup grated Parmigiano-Reggiano

Freshly ground black pepper

12 to 16 squash or pumpkin blossoms

3 cups chicken stock (page 26)

Combine the ricotta, herbs, olive oil, salt, cheese, and pepper, then taste. A spoonful of it should be well seasoned and delicious.

Next, fill the pastry bag (no need for the tip). Spoon the filling into the bag, twist the open end, and give it a squeeze after you've stuck the nose of the tube inside one of the blossoms. The size of the blossoms will vary depending on variety and maturity. That means some will hold lots of the ricotta, while others will just hold a little. Fill each blossom as full as you can, but leave a little room at the top to pinch the ends of the petals together. Don't fuss too much. You'll rip a few, and some will burst a hole in the side. That's okay. You can still use them. Set each stuffed flower aside on a plate until you're just about ready to eat. It's fine to stuff the blossoms ahead and place them in the refrigerator, covered, for an hour or two.

To cook, bring the stock to a simmer in a large sauté pan. Gently set the blossoms in the pan; some will be submerged while others may be as much as half out of the liquid. Set a timer for 2 minutes. Don't flip or turn the delicate blossoms. Instead, spoon a little of the boiling stock over the larger ones as they cook. When the 2 minutes are up, use a slotted spoon or spatula to gently transfer them to your serving plates.

If you have leftover filling, it's delicious mixed into almost any kind of pasta.

Filet Béarnaise
with Potato Wedges and Chopped Fennel Salad

Don't be afraid to make a béarnaise sauce. It's not that hard. Can you ruin it? Will it split? Yes and maybe. But don't think about that. Think about the rich sauce with the infused shallot, wine, and tarragon flavor that finds its perfect match in a rare filet mignon. You *can* do it. Serve with Potato Wedges, so you can dip them in the sauce, Chopped Fennel Salad, and a bottle of red wine you've been saving for a special occasion.

Serves 4

GRILL OR PAN-FRY

4 filets

1 teaspoon kosher salt

Olive oil for rubbing

1 to 2 tablespoons peanut oil for pan-frying

Freshly ground black pepper

BÉARNAISE SAUCE

1 cup unsalted butter

1 shallot, minced

1/4 cup dry white wine

2 tablespoons white wine or champagne vinegar

6 leafy stems tarragon

3 egg yolks

Kosher salt and freshly ground black pepper

Prepare the steaks by salting them, and then let them come to room temperature. Just before cooking, rub with olive oil.

For the sauce, clarify the butter by melting it slowly in a small pot over very low heat—it should not brown. Once it has simmered for several minutes, most of the milk solids will sink and a skin will form on top once the water has fully evaporated. Skim off and discard any cloudy or foamy liquid from the top, then pour off the clear butter slowly. Stop pouring when you reach the milky-white sediment, which you will also discard.

Combine the shallot, wine, vinegar, and half the tarragon stems in a saucepan and reduce to one-third of its original volume, 2 to 3 minutes. Pluck out the spent tarragon and discard. You should have a nice little puddle of liquid along with the translucent shallots. If all your liquid evaporates, add a little more wine or even a tablespoon of water. Transfer the mixture into the top of a double boiler (make sure the bowl is suspended *over,* not touching, the water).

While beating with a whisk, add the egg yolks to your reduction. Continue to beat the mixture until frothy and light. Now, it should begin to heat. This is the crucial moment. If you let the eggs overcook—and you'll know they're doing that if they get really thick—you'll need to start over. What you want to do is catch the mixture before that moment, at the first hint of thickening. When that happens, start adding your butter. Whisk, whisk, whisk and remove from the heat once the butter has been incorporated.

The result should be a smooth, lovely sauce. Strip the remaining 3 sprigs of tarragon of leaves, chop, and toss them in. Mix and taste. Add salt and pepper to taste.

To grill, your coals should be so hot that you can comfortably keep your hand 2 inches above the grate for 3 seconds—just! (For gas grills, this means 450°F.) Put the oiled steaks on the hottest part of the grill and sear for 3 to 5 minutes on each side over high heat before you begin to fuss over them. That means moving the steaks to a cooler part of the grill and cooking for an additional 6 to 10 minutes over moderate heat, flipping, poking, and watching as you work toward crispy-brown perfection. **To pan-fry,** heat the peanut oil in a heavy pan until it's very hot—almost smoking. Sear the steaks for 3 minutes on each side over high heat before turning down the burner. Cook for an additional 6 to 10 minutes over moderate heat, turning every few minutes as they slowly brown. If your kitchen is smoking up like crazy, finish cooking the steaks by putting them, pan and all, in a 400°F oven.

However you cook your steaks, check for doneness often, using the finger-poke method, an instant-read thermometer (120° to 130°F for rare to medium-rare), or the nick-and-peek method (see page 19). Generously salt and pepper each steak before resting them in the warming oven (170°F) or on a warm plate under a loose tent of foil for 5 minutes.

Spoon the béarnaise over the steaks and bring the bowl to the table. Potato Wedges dipped in this buttery sauce are a great thing, so pile them on, slip in some Chopped Fennel Salad, and serve.

Potato Wedges

3 large russet potatoes

2 tablespoons olive oil

Kosher salt and freshly ground black pepper

Preheat the oven to 350°F.

Slice the potatoes into eighths by cutting each in half lengthwise and then the halves into quarters. Toss the cut potatoes with the olive oil to coat each piece evenly. Lay the slices, skin side down, on a cookie sheet. Sprinkle with salt and bake for 40 minutes, or until the ridges of the wedges are brown and the centers are soft when poked with a fork. Add freshly ground pepper and additional salt before serving.

Chopped Fennel Salad

Treat this pretty mix like a condiment; you just need a little on the side of your plate.

2 large fennel bulbs (2 cups chopped)

$1/2$ seedless European cucumber

$1/3$ cup ricotta salata

Juice and zest of $1/2$ lemon (2 tablespoons juice, 1 teaspoon zest)

2 tablespoons your best olive oil

$1/2$ teaspoon kosher salt

Freshly ground black pepper

Peel off the tough outer layer from the fennel by first chopping off the root end and the tips where they begin to split from the main bulb. Reserve the fronds. The interior of the fennel should be a clean, creamy white without any yellow spots or discoloration. Peel another layer off if you must. Starting at the bottom, slice the bulb and then chop into coarse chunks. Slice the cucumber into $1/4$-inch-thick rounds. No need to peel it first. Chop the reserved fennel fronds.

Combine the chopped fronds, fennel bulb, ricotta salata, and cucumber together in a salad bowl and toss with the lemon juice, lemon zest, olive oil, salt, and black pepper. Taste. The salad should be quite lemony and fresh tasting, with a hint of the fruity olive oil.

Steak Tartare
with Grilled Bread and Herb Salad

There's nothing like a crisp bite of toast with cool, velvety steak on top. Steak tartare may be an acquired taste, but many of the best things are—coffee, liver, anchovies. Remember the three key elements for making great steak tartare: 1. Plenty of seasoning; 2. Fresh meat; 3. Top-quality filet. The Herb Salad and Grilled Bread are integral.

Serves 4

HOMEMADE DRESSING
(Makes about 3$1/2$ cups)

4 large egg yolks

$1/2$ cup good white wine vinegar

1 teaspoon salt

4 teaspoons dry mustard

2 cups vegetable oil

$1/2$ cup fruity olive oil

2 cups Homemade Dressing

4 (6-ounce) filets or any combination of steaks totaling 24 ounces

$1/4$ cup capers, minced

$1/4$ cup cornichons, minced

$1/3$ cup parsley, chopped

1 tablespoon plus 1 teaspoon minced anchovy

Kosher salt

Freshly ground white or black pepper

To make the dressing, be sure your eggs aren't icy cold from the refrigerator. Don't let them sit out, but do get them warmed up. I like to heat up a metal mixing bowl with some very hot tap water, thoroughly dry it, and crack the eggs into the warm bowl. By quickly whisking them, they'll pick up a lot of that heat and absorb the oil more easily.

Use a wire whisk to beat the eggs vigorously until they turn a creamy, light yellow. Next, mix in the vinegar, salt, and dry mustard. Integrate both oils by adding just a drizzle while steadily whisking. Continue to add the oil, whisking constantly. Take the process slowly. When you're finished, the consistency will be something like buttermilk.

After you've made your dressing, stick it in the refrigerator—you want to keep the filet and the dressing cold at all times, even between brief lulls in the process. Once you've chopped the capers, cornichons, parsley, and anchovy and set them aside on the counter, you're ready to cut the filet into 1- to 2-inch chunks. Smell the steaks to make sure they're very fresh—the meat should smell clean, without much of a smell at all. Put the filet chunks in the food processor and pulse several times until the meat is evenly ground. Now, add the dressing and on top of that the parsley, capers, cornichons, and anchovies along with a good grind of fresh black or white pepper (white is traditional). Mix gently with a fork just until combined. Taste. It should be fresh tasting, thoroughly seasoned, and delicious. Add more salt as needed. Refrigerate until you're ready to eat.

To serve, have your Grilled Bread and Herb Salad ready. You'll need to chill 4 dinner plates. Do this early so they're very cold. Make a neat pile of the steak tartare on each plate, stack a few pieces of the bread near it, and then load up the salad in the remaining space.

Grilled Bread

Use slices of bread from a sourdough *boule* (*levain*) and a fully flavored fruity young olive oil. If you don't have a grill, use your broiler. Just watch the bread carefully, because it will go from nicely brown to a charred ruin in the time it takes to open a bottle of wine.

6 to 8 slices great bread

3 tablespoons good olive oil

1 teaspoon kosher salt

Drizzle the bread with oil and sprinkle on the salt. To get a bit on both sides, stack up the slices of bread and press them lightly together. Just before you plan to eat, grill the bread over hot embers, watching carefully for burning—this is a great job for a competent guest to take over. Give it time, and don't ever put it over a fresh fire or leaping flames. Done properly, each slice should be just crisp when it's done.

To broil, lay the bread on a cookie sheet in a shape that parallels your broiler element—usually that means two lines down the center of the oven. Put the bread under a preheated broiler; check it after 2 minutes. As silly as it might sound, I like to set a timer. You want the bread to brown without turning black. Leave the bread under the broiler until it's crispy and golden brown.

Herb Salad

This is a very simple salad, with just lemon, salt and pepper, and good olive oil to dress it. The fresh herbs provide spots of bright flavor. Any flavorful, fresh greens will do here. I like Bibb, frisée, and arugula, but the common green leaf or red leaf lettuces, if they're fresh, are also fine. To mix in some color, add radicchio leaves in the winter and nasturtium flowers in the summer.

2 heads lettuce, cleaned

3 sprigs of dill

3 sprigs of parsley

3 sprigs of cilantro

2 tablespoons your best olive oil

Squeeze of lemon

1/2 teaspoon kosher salt

Freshly ground black pepper

Rip the lettuce and the herbs with your hands to create small shreds. I don't like to chop them because the leaves can bruise. Throw all the greens together in a large bowl. Drizzle on the olive oil and lemon juice, add the salt and pepper, and toss. Taste a leaf or two and see whether you need more salt or lemon. The dressing should lightly coat the leaves without weighing them down.

CHAPTER THREE

Latin Steak

A book inspired by skirt steak wouldn't be complete without recipes for fajitas, tacos, and a mole sauce or two. You'll find Southwestern and Latin flavors here, with an emphasis on ingredients like hot peppers, cumin, lime, and cilantro. I begin with the simple Vaquero's Fajita (page 125) of meat, salsa cruda, and roasted peppers; I end with crazy excess of "the works," a jam-packed fajita I named after *Dallas*—the TV show, not the city. In between you'll find recipes for a wide range of steaks from Chipotle-Rubbed Rib Eye with Warm Cilantro-Lime Butter (page 146) to Steak Asado with Chimichurri (page 129). This chapter encompasses Texas and points south, and Cuba and Argentina are represented here, right alongside influences from Belize to Chile.

In the kitchen you'll want skirt steak, plenty of whole cumin, and fresh cilantro. Make sure you have great hot sauce in the house. My mom discovered one called Lottie's, made in Katy, Texas. It's very hot and very good, with a sneaky heat, clean flavor, and not even a hint of vinegar. Marie Sharp's white label sauce is my other favorite. Made in Belize, it'll give you a more mellow heat that you can use freely without worrying about overdoing it.

Nibbles, Starters, and Sweets

Standing around with a margarita in one hand and a guacamole-covered tortilla chip in the other is one of the joys of this kind of food. Why argue with such a fine tradition? Sure, spicy nuts are a good option, too. Make your own by tossing peanuts, pumpkin seeds, or pine nuts—or all three—in a cast-iron pan with a little oil along with crushed pepper flakes, cumin seed, and lime zest. Cook them until they're toasty. They'll wake up your thirst like nothing else can.

Black bean soup, avocado soup, and the classic tortilla soup are all great ways to begin a Latin-influenced meal. Salads that work as first courses are Watermelon–Goat Cheese Salad (page 36) and Radish–Queso Fresco Salad (page 147). Or add some of that queso fresco, along with extra cilantro, avocado, and crushed tortillas, to the Herb Salad (page 119).

If you've never had dulce de leche cake, please try it. It's one of the great ways to end a meal. If you're not up for that, a simple flan is easy and delicious. Make it with pure vanilla, great eggs, and non-ultrapasteurized cream, and you'll be a convert.

Drinks

Beer goes well with this kind of spicy, complex food. Use these steak recipes as an excuse to try new beers from Mexico, Jamaica, Argentina, or somewhere in between.

If you'd rather drink wine (I would), keep in the same spirit and hunt around for something from Latin America. A Malbec, cabernet, or Syrah from Chile or Argentina should have the acidity and tannins to hold up to the lime and spices here. Have fun exploring. Inexpensive and accessible, some of this wine may end up down the sink, but you might also stumble on a bottle you adore at a dreamy price.

Vaquero's Fajita:
Lime-Tequila Marinated Skirt Steak, Roasted Sweet Peppers, and Salsa Cruda

This is the simple cowboy version of the famous fajita—a food that's gotten more bloated and overblown as it's been commercialized (see my excessive version, page 158). With a few sweet peppers, a tortilla, and some grilled meat, there's something deeply satisfying about food this good and this simple.

Serves 4

GRILL OR PAN-FRY

LIME-TEQUILA MARINADE

Juice of 3 limes (about 6 tablespoons)

3 tablespoons tequila

1 teaspoon cumin seed, toasted and ground

2 teaspoons salt

1½ pounds skirt steak

Olive oil for rubbing

1 to 2 tablespoons peanut oil for pan-frying

Kosher salt and freshly ground black pepper

10 corn tortillas, each 6 to 8 inches across

Hot sauce of your choice (optional)

To make the marinade, combine the lime juice, tequila, cumin, and salt in a flat, nonreactive dish (a glass baking dish works great).

Marinate the steak for at least half an hour on the counter-top and up to 24 hours in the refrigerator. When you're ready to cook, fish it out of the marinade and rub it with olive oil.

To grill, your coals should be so hot that you can comfortably keep your hand 2 inches above the grate for 3 seconds—just! (For gas grills, this means 450°F.) Put the oiled steak on the hottest part of the grill and sear for 3 to 5 minutes on each side, then move it over to a lower heat and cook for at most 2 to 5 minutes more—it should always be rare! That's probably all the cooking a skirt steak needs—it cooks fast and gets tough when it's overcooked. **To pan-fry,** heat the peanut oil in your heaviest pan until it's very hot—almost smoking. Sear the steak for 3 minutes on each side over high heat before turning down the burner. Skirt steak will probably be done at this point. If it needs a bit more time, cook over moderate heat for at most 2 to 5 minutes more, turning the steak often as it browns.

Generously salt and pepper the meat before resting it in a warming oven (170°F) or on a warm plate under a loose tent of foil for 5 minutes.

While the meat is resting, put your tortillas on the grill. You're mostly just heating them, but a little browning is a nice side effect. Cook for 2 to 3 minutes and then wrap in foil to keep them warm. (You can also cook the tortillas over the burner on a gas stove; use tongs to keep flipping them.)

Before serving, slice the steak across the grain into long strips. Serve the meat, Roasted Sweet Peppers, and Salsa Cruda with the warm tortillas and let people make their own fajitas. Add a drop of hot sauce if you like it that way.

Roasted Sweet Peppers

I like to combine two or three colors of peppers for contrast. Yellow, red, and orange are great—don't use green, which have a very different flavor.

2 sweet bell peppers, seeded and cut into eighths

1 tablespoon good olive oil

1/2 teaspoon kosher salt

Preheat the oven to 400°F. Put the pepper slices on a sheet pan, drizzle on the oil, and toss to coat. Spread the slices out, sprinkle them with salt, and put them in the oven for 20 minutes. Turn them occasionally so they brown evenly. You want them to be sweet and soft but still juicy.

Salsa Cruda

This is a simple, chunky salsa you won't fuss over. There's no need to measure every ingredient with the precision of a baker—go with your instincts and make it to your taste. Use the best tomatoes you can find. Sometimes cherry tomatoes are the safest bet, but in late July and August there's nothing better than the heirloom varieties from your garden or local farmers' market.

1¹/₂ cups diced tomato

1/2 cup cilantro, chopped

3 breakfast radishes, diced

1/2 jalapeño, seeded and minced (about 2 tablespoons)

1/2 small onion, peeled and chopped (about 1/2 cup)

1/2 teaspoon salt

1 teaspoon lime juice

1 clove garlic, peeled and minced

Gut the tomatoes by cutting them in half and squeezing the juice out. *Then* chop the flesh. Combine all the ingredients in a small mixing bowl and stir. This salsa benefits from sitting for an hour, which allows the flavors to blend and mellow. Taste and make sure it has enough salt for the fullest flavor.

Steak Asado:
Chimichurri, Diced Avocado, and Lime Wedges with Corn Griddle Cakes

This classic Argentine sauce is good on almost anything, and its vibrant green color is a joy to look at. I run everything on my plate around in it: steak, Corn Griddle Cakes, and Black Beans (page 135)—if I have them. I try to save enough sauce for breakfast so I can put some on my eggs. (It's hangover food for the gods.)

Serves 4
GRILL OR PAN-FRY

1 large porterhouse (about 2 pounds)

1 teaspoon salt
Olive oil for rubbing
1 to 2 tablespoons peanut oil for pan-frying
Freshly ground black pepper

CHIMICHURRI
2 cloves garlic, cut into quarters
1 cup cilantro leaves
1 cup mint leaves
1 cup parsley leaves
1 teaspoon salt
1/2 teaspoon cayenne
1/2 cup extra virgin olive oil

1 Hass avocado
Squeeze of lime juice

Prepare the steak by salting it, then let it come to room temperature. Rub with a bit of olive oil just before cooking.

To make the chimichurri, combine the garlic, cilantro, mint, parsley, salt, and cayenne in a food processor and blend. Once everything is pulverized, slowly add the oil, allowing it to blend thoroughly. Pour the sauce into a bowl and set aside at room temperature. (You can also use a mortar and pestle to make this sauce.)

Pit the avocado by slicing it in half lengthwise. Now that you have two halves, cut the flesh in each from top to bottom, 6 to 8 times. While the avocado is still in its skin, cut each slice across to create cubes. Run your fingers along the skin on the inside to release the cubes into a bowl, and immediately toss them with the lime juice.

To grill, your coals should be so hot that you can comfortably keep your hand 2 inches above the grate for 3 seconds—just! (For gas grills, this means 450°F.) Put the oiled steak on the hottest part of the grill and sear for 3 to 5 minutes on each side over high heat before you begin to fuss over it. That means moving the steak to a cooler part of the grill and cooking for an additional 8 to 12 minutes over moderate heat, flipping, poking, and watching as you work toward crispy-brown perfection. **To pan-fry,** heat the peanut oil in a heavy pan until it's very hot—almost smoking. Sear the steak for 3 minutes on each side over high heat before turning down the burner. Cook for an additional 8 to 12 minutes over moderate heat, turning it every few minutes as it slowly browns. For steak more than 2 inches thick, you may want to finish cooking it by putting it, pan and all, in a 400°F oven.

However you cook your steak, check for doneness often, using the finger-poke method, an instant-read thermometer (120° to 130°F for rare to medium-rare), or the nick-and-peek method (see page 19). Generously salt and pepper each steak before resting it in a warming oven (170°F) or on a warm plate under a loose tent of foil for 5 minutes.

To serve, pour a pool of the chimichurri sauce onto each warm plate or use one large platter. Slice the steak and make a neat pile of diced avocado on top of the meat. Bring the Corn Griddle Cakes to the table separately or add one to each plate. The leftover sauce should go on the table.

Corn Griddle Cakes

These simple pancakes are made in the spirit of the venerable street food, the *arrepa*—a corn pancake and cheese sandwich. Unlike an *arrepa*, though, this one has no cheese and no sugar in the batter. Make these cakes with fresh corn if possible; frozen corn should be briefly cooked and drained.

1 cup milk

4 tablespoons unsalted butter, melted

2 ears corn, kernels shaved off

2 eggs

1 cup cornmeal

1/2 cup flour

1 1/2 teaspoons kosher salt

1 teaspoon baking soda

Oil or butter for the griddle

In a mixing bowl, combine the milk, melted butter, and corn kernels. Add the eggs, beating with a wire whisk. When thoroughly blended, add the cornmeal, flour, salt, and baking soda. Mix the batter with a rubber spatula, not a whisk. Avoid overworking the batter; a few brisk stirs with a rubber spatula should be enough.

Heat a griddle over medium-high heat and then add a little oil or butter. The oil should be hot but not smoking. Do a small test cake—when it browns nicely, the griddle is ready. Ladle on small pools of batter to make saucer-size cakes (4-inch rounds). Cook both sides until golden brown and crispy around the edges. Sprinkle with kosher salt and transfer the cakes to a warming oven (170°F).

Cuban-Style Seville Orange–Marinated Skirt Steak with Rum-Glazed Plantains and Black Beans

This is a *mojo*, really. Whatever you call it, this sauce goes with beans, steak, and lime-based rum drinks. So, make up some of this marinade that doubles as a sauce, put a pot of Black Beans on the stove, and fire up the grill for the steak and the Rum-Glazed Plantains. While you wait for the grill, don't be shy about stirring up an icy pitcher of fresh lime juice, simple syrup, and dark rum.

If you can't find Seville oranges, which are only available in December and January, you can buy a jar of what's often called sour orange juice. You can also squeeze a cup of fresh Valencia orange juice and add 3 tablespoons of lemon juice. I prefer the latter.

Serves 4

GRILL OR PAN-FRY

SEVILLE ORANGE MARINADE

1 cup freshly squeezed Seville orange juice

3 cloves garlic, peeled and crushed

1 teaspoon cumin seed, toasted and ground

$1/2$ teaspoon kosher salt

1 jalapeño or Scotch bonnet, seeded and minced

3 tablespoons olive oil

2 pounds skirt steak, hangar steak, or top blade steak

Olive oil for rubbing

1 to 2 tablespoons peanut oil for pan-frying

Kosher salt and freshly ground black pepper

To make the marinade, which is doubling as both a marinade and a sauce, combine the orange juice, garlic, cumin, salt, chile pepper, and olive oil in a shallow nonreactive baking dish.

Add the steak and flip to coat. Allow it to marinate at room temperature for 1 hour or for up to 24 hours in the refrigerator. When you're almost ready to cook the meat, take it out of the marinade (reserve the marinade) and rub it with olive oil.

Pour the reserved marinade into a small saucepan and bring it to a boil. Simmer to reduce by half (10 to 15 minutes). Add salt and pepper to taste. This makes an unassuming, not-too-sweet sauce for the meat. (It is essential to boil the marinade for at least 5 minutes to get rid of any possible bacteria from the raw meat.)

To grill, your coals should be so hot that you can comfortably keep your hand 2 inches above the grate for 3 seconds—just! (For gas grills, this means 450°F.) Put the oiled steak on the hottest part of the grill and sear for 3 to 5 minutes on each side over high heat. For skirt steak, that should be all the cooking the meat needs; if it needs a bit more, cook at most 2 to 5 minutes more over lower heat—it should always be rare! **To pan-fry,** heat the peanut oil in a heavy pan until it's very hot—almost smoking. Sear the steak for 3 minutes on each side over high heat before turning down the burner. Again, 3 minutes a side is probably enough for skirt steak. If it needs a bit more time, cook for at most 2 to 5 minutes more, turning it often as it browns.

However you cook your steak, check for doneness often, using the finger-poke or the nick-and-peek method (see page 19). Generously salt and pepper the steak before resting it in a warming oven (170°F) or on a warm plate under a loose tent of foil for 5 minutes.

After resting, slice the steak the long way—against its natural grain, creating the longest strips you can. Spoon a pool of sauce onto each warm plate, distribute the steak among the plates, and add a piece of plantain and a generous scoop of black beans. Make sure there's hot sauce on the table.

Rum-Glazed Plantains

You want plantains that are yellow-black. If they're very ripe, they won't hold up on the grill; if they're very green, they'll need to cook a lot longer and they won't be as sweet. To peel very green plantains, slit them and blanch them. Then peel.

$^1/_2$ cup dark rum (Goslings Black Seal from Bermuda is pretty great)

$^1/_2$ cup firmly packed brown sugar

2 tablespoons butter

2 medium-ripe plantains

Kosher salt

Combine the rum, sugar, and 1 tablespoon of the butter in a small pot over medium heat. Bring to a boil, reduce the heat, and allow the sauce to simmer. The sugar will dissolve and the rum will begin to evaporate. Cook for 5 to 10 minutes to reduce by one-third. Take the pot off the heat and set it aside. The sauce will thicken a little.

Peel the plantains and cut the flesh into quarters, once in half the long way and once across the length. Smear the plantains with the remaining 1 tablespoon of butter and a pinch of salt and put them on the grill. Let them cook gently over medium-hot coals until they soften and begin to brown. When you think they're almost cooked, begin painting on the rum glaze with a brush. Grill for another couple of minutes, continuing to coat them on all sides. Be careful to avoid burning them at this point, which they will do easily because of the sugar in the glaze. You do want that sugar to caramelize a little, though. As soon as you smell the browning sugar, take them off.

Black Beans

1 pound dried black beans
(a little more than 2 cups)

6 slices bacon

3 onions, coarsely chopped
(about 2 cups)

1 jalapeño, seeded and
chopped (optional)

5 cloves garlic, coarsely
chopped

1 tablespoon cumin seeds,
toasted and ground

2 teaspoons kosher salt

Rinse the beans, looking for stray rocks, and then cover with water and soak overnight. Cover the beans generously with water since they will absorb quite a bit in the first few hours. If you didn't plan this far ahead, that's okay. Move on to the next step and expect a longer cooking time.

Whether you've soaked the beans or not, rinse them with fresh water and put them in a big heavy pot on the stove along with enough water to fully cover them. With a lid on, but slightly ajar, cook the beans on the lowest setting for 2 to 3 hours, or until tender (unsoaked beans can take 4 hours). You'll need to stir them occasionally and add water as needed. You want them to be soft but still hold their shape.

When the beans are just about done, cook the bacon in a large frying pan until crisp. Remove the slices to drain on a paper towel and pour off as much of the fat as you like. I like to keep most of it; reserve at least a slick. Add the onions to the hot pan and cook in the bacon fat. Gently cook until soft, about 10 minutes. Add the jalapeño, garlic, cumin, and salt and cook, stirring, for another 5 minutes. Combine with the beans. Taste for salt and heat.

Strip Steak with Tequila-Avocado Sauce,
Roasted Chayote Squash, and Quinoa Salad

I know this all looks a bit difficult and fancy, but that's because the ingredients seem exotic because they're unfamiliar. This sauce has the intense flavor with the richness of avocados while avoiding the guacamole-on-a-steak effect you might expect. The citrusy freshness of tomatillos with the final finish of the juices from the resting steaks is what makes it so good. The Roasted Chayote Squash is juicy and succulent—not mushy or sweet. It's a perfect antidote to the lavish richness of the sauce. And Quinoa Salad is a welcome change from rice, providing freshness and a spicy bite.

Serves 4
GRILL OR PAN-FRY

4 strip steaks, bone-in or boneless

1 teaspoon kosher salt

Olive oil for rubbing

1 to 2 tablespoons peanut oil for pan-frying

Freshly ground black pepper

TEQUILA-AVOCADO SAUCE

1/2 cup chopped tomatillos (about 3)

1/2 teaspoon hot sauce

1/2 teaspoon salt

1 clove garlic, peeled and crushed

1/4 cup cilantro leaves, coarsely chopped

1/2 Hass avocado

Juice of 1 lime (3 tablespoons or so)

2 tablespoons best-quality tequila

Grape tomatoes or the smallest you can find, sliced in half, for garnish

Prepare the steaks by salting them, then let them come to room temperature. Rub thoroughly with a bit of olive oil just before cooking.

To make the sauce, peel the papery husks from the tomatillos, and then drop them in a pot of boiling water for 3 minutes. This brings out their flavor, removes the sticky residue, and softens them. After cooking, rinse with cold water to stop the cooking. Core as you would a normal tomato. Put the tomatillos in a food processor, along with the hot sauce, salt, garlic, cilantro leaves, avocado, lime juice, and tequila. Blend until smooth. Set the sauce aside to finish after the steaks are done.

To grill, your coals should be so hot that you can comfortably keep your hand 2 inches above the grate for 3 seconds—just! (For gas grills, this means 450°F.) Put the oiled steaks on the hottest part of the grill and sear for 3 to 5 minutes on each side over intense heat before you begin to fuss over them. That means moving the steaks to a cooler part of the grill and cooking gently over more moderate heat for an additional 6 to 10 minutes, flipping, poking, and watching as you work toward crispy-brown perfection. **To pan-fry,** heat the peanut oil in a heavy pan until it's very hot—almost smoking. Sear the steaks for 3 minutes on each side over high heat before turning down the burner. Cook over moderate heat for an additional 6 to 10 minutes, turning the steaks every few minutes as they slowly brown. For steaks more than 2 inches thick, you may want to finish cooking them by putting them, pan and all, in a 400°F oven.

However you cook your steaks, check for doneness often, using the finger-poke method, an instant-read thermometer

(120° to 130°F for rare to medium-rare), or the nick-and-peek method (see page 19). Generously salt and pepper each steak before resting it in a warming oven (170°F) or on a warm plate under a loose tent of foil for 5 minutes.

While the steaks rest, finish the sauce. Sneak any juices from the resting meat and whisk them together with the avocado sauce in a frying pan. Cook over high heat to reduce slightly, about 3 minutes. Put just a little of the sauce onto each steak, scattering with the sliced tomatoes, and add a slice of squash and some Quinoa Salad to each plate. Any remaining sauce should be put on the table.

Roasted Chayote Squash

1 chayote squash, skin on
1 tablespoon olive oil
1 teaspoon salt
Pinch of cayenne pepper

Preheat the oven to 350°F. Slice the squash into 8 pieces, as you would an apple. No need to seed or core them. Just trim off the stem. Toss to coat with the olive oil, sprinkle with salt and cayenne, and roast for half an hour, or until the pieces begin to brown. Flip the slices over after 15 minutes so the pieces cook evenly.

Quinoa Salad

1 cup quinoa

2 cups water

1/2 teaspoon kosher salt

2 cups arugula leaves

1/2 cup chopped cherry tomatoes (20 grape tomatoes)

1 tablespoon chopped mint

1 tablespoon chopped fresh oregano leaves

1 tablespoon chopped parsley

3 radishes, sliced into thin rounds

3 scallions, finely chopped (2 tablespoons)

2 tablespoons your best olive oil

1 tablespoon white vinegar

Freshly ground black pepper

1/4 cup French feta or queso fresco (I prefer feta)

Bring the quinoa, water, and salt to boil in a lidded pot over medium heat. Once it boils, reduce the heat, stir, cover, and simmer for 15 to 20 minutes. Like rice, quinoa is done when the water has been absorbed and the grain is tender. Set aside to cool.

In a large salad bowl, combine the arugula, tomatoes, mint, oregano, parsley, radishes, and scallions. In a separate bowl, combine the olive oil, vinegar, and salt and pepper to taste, and toss the salad with it. Gently scatter the quinoa and feta on the salad mix before serving.

Rib Steak with Orange Bell Pepper Puree,
Cilantro, Pine Nuts, and Fingerling Potatoes

Bright orange with black flecks, this puree puts the sweet, smoky taste of roasted pepper right on your steak. The cilantro and pine nuts add complexity and texture, but the secret ingredient here is a mild but flavorful hot sauce such as Marie Sharp's (see Pantry section). I like some Fingerling Potatoes and a cold beer with this meal.

Serves 4

GRILL OR PAN-FRY

4 rib steaks

1 teaspoon kosher salt

Olive oil for rubbing

1 to 2 tablespoons peanut oil for pan-frying

Freshly ground black pepper

ORANGE BELL PEPPER PUREE

1 orange bell pepper, halved and seeded

5 tablespoons olive oil

1 tablespoon Marie Sharp's habanero sauce

1 teaspoon kosher salt

1/4 cup cilantro leaves

1/4 cup pine nuts

Prepare the steaks by salting them, then let them come to room temperature. Rub with olive oil before cooking.

To make the puree, using your hands, coat the bell pepper with some of the olive oil. To blacken it, place both halves skin side up under your broiler or, if you're grilling, skin side to the fire on the grill. You want to blacken the skin and, at the same time, bring out the pepper's sweetness by cooking it. Once it's at least partly blackened, slice it up and put it in a food processor along with the remaining oil, the hot sauce, and the salt. If you don't have Marie Sharp's, use any reasonably mild, low-acid hot sauce. Blend until smooth.

To grill, your coals should be so hot that you can comfortably keep your hand 2 inches above the grate for 3 seconds—just! (For gas grills, this means 450°F.) Put the oiled steaks on the hottest part of the grill and sear for 3 to 5 minutes on each side before you begin to fuss over them. That means moving the steaks to a cooler part of the grill and cooking for an additional 8 to 12 minutes over moderate heat, flipping, poking, and watching as you work toward crispy-brown perfection.

To pan-fry, heat the peanut oil in a heavy pan until it's very hot—almost smoking. Sear the steaks for 3 minutes on each side over high heat before turning down the burner. Cook over moderate heat for an additional 8 to 12 minutes, turning the steaks every few minutes as they slowly brown. For steaks more than 2 inches thick, you may want to finish cooking them by putting them, pan and all, in a 400°F oven.

However you cook your steaks, check for doneness often, using the finger-poke method, an instant-read thermometer (120° to130°F for rare to medium-rare), or the nick-and-peek method (see page 19). Generously salt and pepper each steak before resting them in a warming oven (170°F) or on a warm plate under a loose tent of foil for 5 minutes.

Chop the cilantro leaves and toast the nuts in a small cast-iron pan or in the oven. They should be just beginning to color and become fragrant. Put the steaks on warm plates with some of the vivid orange puree on top. The cilantro leaves can be casually strewn about along with a generous pinch of pine nuts. A few potatoes and the plate is ready.

Fingerling Potatoes

These potatoes rely on the flavor of a fresh, intense, slightly peppery unfiltered green olive oil and a potato that is either recently dug or has been carefully stored. Whether they're fingerlings or just small round potatoes, avoid those with sprouts and be prepared with a worthy olive oil (see the Pantry section at the end of the book).

1 pound fingerling potatoes
(I like Russian Banana, French, and Rose Finn Apple)

1 tablespoon your best olive oil

3 tablespoons chopped parsley

1 teaspoon kosher salt

Freshly ground black pepper

Steam the potatoes until tender, about 20 minutes for most varieties, depending on the size. Use a fork to test for doneness. Transfer to a bowl, drizzle on the oil, and toss with the parsley, salt, and black pepper. Taste and salt again as needed.

Porterhouse with Black Mexican Chocolate Sauce and Pan Corn

This excellent sauce is made with smoky chiles and dark chocolate. It's essentially a mole, which explains the litany of nuts, spices, and chiles. The finished sauce has the color of Moab Desert dirt. It's great with Pan Corn and Black Beans (page 135).

Mexican chocolate is pretty widely available now, but I prefer bittersweet chocolate with plenty of cocoa solids—60 percent and up. This will give you potent chocolate flavor with little of the sweetness.

Serves 4

GRILL OR PAN-FRY

1 large porterhouse (about 2 pounds)

1 tablespoon kosher salt

Olive oil for rubbing

1 to 2 tablespoons peanut oil for pan-frying

Freshly ground black pepper

BLACK MEXICAN CHOCOLATE SAUCE

1 dried pasilla chile, seeded and chopped (reserve the seeds)

2 chipotles in adobo sauce, seeded and chopped

1 cup cooked black beans

1 ounce dark chocolate, coarsely chopped

1/3 cup almonds, toasted

1 teaspoon kosher salt

2 cups chicken stock (page 26)

2 tablespoons olive oil

1 clove garlic, peeled and crushed

2 shallots, peeled and coarsely chopped (about 1/3 cup)

Prepare the steak by salting it, then let it come to room temperature. Rub with a bit of olive oil just before cooking.

Rehydrate the pasilla chile by pouring boiling water over it and allowing it to soak for half an hour. When you're ready to make the sauce, pull the chile open and seed it. Chop coarsely and put in a blender or food processor with the chipotles, black beans, chocolate, almonds, and salt. Blend, adding the stock slowly, allowing the blades to do their work as the sauce thins out.

Heat the olive oil in a sauté pan and gently sauté the garlic and shallots over low heat. Once they're soft, add them to the blended chile-chocolate mix and blend again. Transfer the sauce to a saucepan and simmer for 10 minutes. Keep an eye on it to avoid scalding—the chocolate and nuts are delicate. Taste. It should have a subtle but definite heat and enough salt to bring out the diverse flavors. If the sauce needs to be spicier, add some of the reserved chile seeds, ground with a mortar and pestle, or you could add some low-acid hot sauce such as Lottie's or Marie Sharp's.

To grill, your coals should be so hot that you can comfortably keep your hand 2 inches above the grate for 3 seconds—just! (For gas grills, this means 450°F.) Put the oiled steak on the hottest part of the grill and sear for 3 to 5 minutes on each side over high heat before you begin to fuss over it. That means moving the steak to a cooler part of the grill and cooking for an additional 8 to 12 minutes over moderate heat, flipping, poking, and watching as you work toward crispy-brown perfection. **To pan-fry,** heat the peanut oil in a heavy pan until it's very hot—almost smoking. Sear the steak for 3 minutes on each side over high heat before turning down the burner. Cook over moderate heat for an additional 8 to 12 minutes, turning the steak every few minutes as it slowly browns. For steak more than 2 inches thick, you may want to finish cooking it by putting it, pan and all, in a 400°F oven.

However you cook your steak, check for doneness often, using the finger-poke method, an instant-read thermometer (120° to 130°F for rare to medium-rare), or the nick-and-peek method (see page 19). Generously salt and pepper each steak before resting them in a warming oven (170°F) or on a warm plate under a loose tent of foil for 5 minutes.

Make a small pool of the sauce on each plate and then place a steak on top of it. Add plenty of Pan Corn to each plate. Have the extra mole sauce on the table.

Pan Corn

4 slices thick-cut bacon

2 leeks, the bottom third sliced into rounds

4 ears sweet corn, kernels shaved off the cob

Kosher salt and freshly ground black pepper

Cook the bacon in a heavy frying pan until it's crisp. Transfer to a rack or paper towel to drain, then chop when it's cool. Pour off all but 1 tablespoon of the bacon fat from the bacon pan and add the leeks, cooking them gently until soft. Add the corn kernels and the bacon. Allow the corn to cook for a few minutes, depending on how fresh it is—very fresh local corn takes only a minute. Taste for salt, grind on a good bit of fresh black pepper, and eat.

Truck Tacos:
Skirt Steak, Queso Fresco, and Corn Salsa

These tacos are inspired by the funky taco trucks that dot the landscape in Mexico, where I traveled a lot as a kid. Next to a tamale stand, there's no sweeter sight on the horizon. The trifecta would be to run into both at once, along with a stand that sold iced beer out of a cooler. There's nothing like eating something so ridiculously good by the side of the road. And all for a buck or two. They taste pretty great at home, too. You don't want to overthink a taco. Still, salsa from a jar is fatal to the spirit (and taste) of these tacos. If you can't find queso fresco, then French feta or a mild crumbled goat cheese will do the trick.

Serves 4

GRILL OR PAN-FRY

1½ pounds skirt steak

1 recipe Lime-Tequila Marinade (page 125)

Olive oil for rubbing

2 tablespoons peanut oil for pan-frying

Freshly ground black pepper

CORN SALSA

1 cup corn kernels, fresh or frozen

2 tomatoes

2 cloves garlic

2 tablespoons lime juice (1 lime)

6 scallions, bottom third thinly sliced

½ cup cilantro, chopped

1 teaspoon kosher salt

1 jalapeño or other hot chile, minced and seeded

½ teaspoon Marie Sharp's or other hot sauce (optional)

10 small corn tortillas (6 to 8 inches across)

Queso fresco, crumbled or chopped into small chunks

Put the steak flat in a glass or ceramic baking pan and add the Lime-Tequila Marinade, flipping it to coat. Marinate the meat for an hour at room temperature, or for up to 24 hours in the refrigerator. Before cooking, rub the steak with olive oil.

To make the salsa, in a small saucepan, boil the corn kernels in lightly salted water for 1 minute if fresh and 3 minutes if frozen. Drain the corn and let cool. Core and then gut the tomatoes by slicing them in half and giving them a good squeeze to remove the excess juices. Coarsely chop the tomatoes. Either chop the garlic or use a press to get it very fine. Combine the corn, tomatoes, garlic, lime juice, scallions, cilantro, salt, jalapeño, and hot sauce in a small bowl and stir.

Preheat the oven to 300°F. If you have your grill going, toast the tortillas on it. If not, and you have a gas stove, put the tortillas on the burner, right over a medium-high flame. Use tongs to move them around. Giving them this burner treatment crisps them up a little; don't worry about black spots here and there. When you've finished doing them all, wrap them tightly in foil and stick them in the oven. If you don't have a gas stove, just put the tortillas in the oven, tightly wrapped in foil, for 20 minutes.

To grill, your coals should be so hot that you can comfortably keep your hand 2 inches above the grate for 3 seconds— just! (For gas grills, this means 450°F.) Put the oiled steak on the hottest part of the grill and sear for 3 to 5 minutes on each side over high heat. If your fire is hot enough, it should be done; if it needs a bit more time, move it over to a lower heat and cook for at most 2 to 5 minutes more—skirt steak should always be rare! **To pan-fry,** heat the peanut oil in a heavy pan until it's very hot—almost smoking. Sear the steak for

1/4 cup cilantro leaves, chopped

2 avocados, sliced and salted

Kosher salt

Hot sauce

3 minutes on each side over high heat before turning down the burner. Cook over moderate heat for at most 2 to 5 more minutes, turning the steak often as it browns. It should be done.

However you cook your steak, test for doneness often, using the finger-poke or the nick-and-peek method (see page 19). Skirt steak cooks fast and gets tough if you overcook it. Generously salt and pepper the steak before resting it in a warming oven (170°F) or on a warm plate under a loose tent of foil for 5 minutes.

Slice the steak along its length, against the grain, creating long, thin strips. Take your tortillas out of the oven and begin assembling the tacos. I like to start with two per person and then go back for more if I want (I always do). Divide the meat among the tortillas. Spread on a couple spoonfuls of salsa, a sprinkling of queso fresco, and some chopped cilantro leaves. Tuck in a few slices of avocado and then give the whole thing a pinch of kosher salt and a dab of hot sauce. Fold and eat.

A cold Tecate beer and a fresh napkin later and you'll be ready for another.

Chipotle-Rubbed Rib Eye
with Warm Lime-Cilantro Butter, Spanish Rice, and Radish–Queso Fresco Salad

This is a bold steak—it packs a wallop of smoke and spice. The bright cilantro butter sauce brings a nice hit of acid with the herbal dose of the cilantro to round out the chipotle's smoky-chocolate flavor. Add a cold beer, Spanish Rice to run around in the butter, and Radish–Queso Fresco Salad. Of course, there's always tequila . . .

Serves 4

GRILL OR PAN-FRY

CHIPOTLE RUB

1/2 teaspoon whole cumin seed, toasted

1 teaspoon kosher salt

1 teaspoon ground red chipotle

2 pounds rib eye, either 4 individual steaks or 2 large steaks to slice

1 tablespoon olive oil

1 to 2 tablespoons peanut oil for pan-frying

Kosher salt and freshly ground black pepper

LIME-CILANTRO BUTTER

4 tablespoons butter

1 shallot, minced

1/2 lime, juiced (about 2 tablespoons)

1/2 cup cilantro, finely chopped

To make the rub, grind the cumin with a mortar and pestle, then combine it with the salt and chipotle powder. Rub the spice mix on the meat and then rub on the olive oil. Let the steaks come to room temperature before cooking.

Melt the butter in a sauté pan over very low heat and add the shallot. Cook for 2 to 3 minutes, just long enough to soften the shallot. Add the lime juice and cilantro and stir. Turn off the heat and set the sauce aside.

To grill, your coals should be so hot that you can comfortably keep your hand 2 inches above the grate for 3 seconds—just! (For gas grills, this means 450°F.) Put the oiled steaks on the hottest part of the grill and sear for 3 to 5 minutes on each side over high heat before you begin to fuss over them. That means moving the steaks to a cooler part of the grill and cooking for an additional 8 to 12 minutes over moderate heat, flipping, poking, and watching as you work toward crispy-brown perfection. **To pan-fry,** heat the peanut oil in a heavy pan until it's very hot—almost smoking. Sear the steaks for 3 minutes on each side over high heat before turning down the burner. Cook for an additional 8 to 12 minutes over moderate heat, turning the steaks often as they slowly brown. For steaks more than 2 inches thick, you may want to finish cooking them by putting them, pan and all, in a 400°F oven.

However you cook your steak, check for doneness often, using the finger-poke method, an instant-read thermometer (120° to 130°F for rare to medium-rare), or the nick-and-peek method (see page 19). Rest the steaks in a warming oven (170°F) or on a warm plate under a loose tent of foil for 5 minutes. Give the steaks a final dose of salt and a grind of fresh black pepper before pouring on the sauce.

Spanish Rice

Turmeric has been around for ages. Its potent pigments make it invaluable—and not just in the kitchen. Buy it fresh and use it often. Seek out good tomatoes for the biggest flavor—cherry tomatoes are often the best bet in winter.

2 cups long-grain rice (basmati is my favorite)

3 tablespoons olive oil

1½ teaspoons kosher salt

1½ cups chopped tomato

1 teaspoon turmeric

¼ teaspoon cayenne pepper

1 clove garlic, minced

1 red onion, chopped

4 cups unsalted chicken stock (page 26)

In a large saucepan with a lid, combine the rice, oil, salt, tomato, turmeric, cayenne, garlic, and onion. Stir, over medium heat, to toast the rice and soften the onion. Keep it moving for 3 to 5 minutes before adding the stock. Cook, covered, for 20 minutes, or until the stock is absorbed and the rice is tender. Take a taste—it should be subtly spicy.

Radish–Queso Fresco Salad

I like this simple salad with spicy food because it has its own natural bite but delivers a terrific, cooling crunch. But then, I love radishes in almost any form.

2 cups breakfast or other radishes, trimmed

2 ounces queso fresco or French feta

Kosher salt and freshly ground black pepper

1 tablespoon good olive oil

Slice the radishes into rounds, crumble on the cheese, add a few grinds of pepper, and then drizzle on the oil. Toss thoroughly and taste for salt—you may not need any.

Caribbean Spice Paste–Rubbed Top Sirloin
with Lime-Cilantro Crema and Red Beans and Rice

This potent spice rub is mellowed by the cool lime crema. It also goes great with the Red Beans and Rice, which are made with a hint of cinnamon, coconut, and the kick of a Scotch bonnet pepper. A cool island rum drink would be appropriate.

Serves 4

GRILL OR PAN-FRY

CARIBBEAN SPICE PASTE

1 teaspoon red pepper flakes

1 tablespoon Mexican oregano

2 cloves garlic, peeled and crushed

2 teaspoons cumin seeds, toasted

$^1/_2$ teaspoon cinnamon

1 teaspoon kosher salt

1 teaspoon coriander seeds

1 teaspoon paprika

2 tablespoons olive oil

2 pounds top sirloin

1 to 2 tablespoons peanut oil for pan-frying

Kosher salt and freshly ground black pepper

LIME-CILANTRO CREMA

1 cup full-fat sour cream

2 tablespoons lime juice (1 lime)

$^1/_4$ cup cilantro, chopped

To make the spice paste, combine the pepper flakes, oregano, garlic, cumin seeds, cinnamon, salt, coriander, and paprika in a mortar and grind until pulverized. Add the olive oil and work the mixture into a paste. Using your hands, smear the steaks with the paste, coating them as evenly as possible. Let the meat come to room temperature.

To make the Lime-Cilantro Crema, simply combine the sour cream, lime juice, and cilantro and stir. Cover and refrigerate until needed.

To grill, your coals should be so hot that you can comfortably hold your hand 2 inches above the grate for 3 seconds—just! (For gas grills, this means 450°F.) Put the oiled steaks on the hottest part of the grill and sear for 3 to 5 minutes on each side before you begin to fuss over them. That means moving the steaks to a cooler part of the grill and cooking for an additional 6 to 10 minutes over moderate heat, flipping, poking, and watching as you work toward crispy-brown perfection. **To pan-fry,** heat the peanut oil in a heavy pan until it's very hot—almost smoking. Sear the steaks for 3 minutes on each side over high heat before turning down the burner. Cook over moderate heat for an additional 6 to 10 minutes, turning the steaks often as they slowly brown. If your house is filling with smoke, finish cooking the steaks by putting them, pan and all, in a 400°F oven.

However you cook your steaks, check for doneness often, using the finger-poke method, an instant-read thermometer (120° to 130°F for rare to medium-rare), or the nick-and-peek method (see page 19). Generously salt and pepper each steak before letting them rest in a warming oven (170°F) or on a warm plate under a loose tent of foil for 5 minutes.

This makes a simple, unassuming plate: Slice the steak, add some Red Beans and Rice, and finish with a dollop of the Lime-Cilantro Crema.

Red Beans and Rice

1½ cups dried red kidney beans

4 slices bacon

1 red onion, chopped

½ Scotch bonnet pepper, seeded and chopped

1 teaspoon kosher salt

½ teaspoon ground cinnamon

½ teaspoon allspice

2 cups unsweetened coconut milk

1 cup rice

4 scallions, trimmed and bottom third chopped

Soak the beans overnight in cold water or pour boiling water to cover and allow them to sit for 1 hour before rinsing. Put the beans in a heavy pot and cover them with fresh water. Cover the pot and cook, over low heat, for 1½ to 2 hours. Stir, skim, and add more liquid as needed. When the beans are nearly cooked and the liquid has been absorbed, turn off the heat. In a sauté pan, fry the bacon until crisp. Retain the grease and cook the onion and pepper for 5 minutes, or until just soft. Add the bacon, onion, and pepper to the beans, along with the salt, cinnamon, allspice, coconut milk, and rice. Cook, covered, over very low heat for another 20 minutes, or until the coconut milk is absorbed and the rice is tender. Stir often to prevent scorching. Taste, adding salt as needed, and serve garnished with chopped scallions.

Flank Steak
with Oaxacan Mole Verde Sauce and Baked Tortillas

This is a vibrant sauce that calls for a litany of ingredients. Don't be daunted! It's not so hard, and you'll have something to eat that's new and delicious. Simple and unobtrusive, the Baked Tortillas effortlessly pair up with big flavors while still holding their own quiet corner on satisfaction.

This recipe makes a little more sauce than you'll need. Freeze it or mix it with some slow-cooked pork the next day.

Serves 4

GRILL OR PAN-FRY

2 pounds flank steak

1 teaspoon kosher salt

Olive oil for rubbing

1 to 2 tablespoons peanut oil for pan-frying

Freshly ground black pepper

Cilantro leaves, coarsely chopped, for garnish

OAXACAN MOLE VERDE SAUCE

5 tomatillos

1 corn tortilla, 6 to 8 inches across

1/2 onion, cut into chunks

1/4 ripe plantain, sliced vertically

1 fresh serrano chile, seeded and seeds reserved

1 fresh jalapeño, seeded and seeds reserved

Olive oil for roasting

1/4 cup raw peanuts

12 raw almonds

12 walnut halves

1 tablespoon raw sesame seeds

1 teaspoon cumin seeds

1/4 teaspoon aniseed

Prepare the steak by salting it, and then let it come to room temperature. Rub with olive oil just before cooking.

To make the sauce, preheat the oven to 450°F. Begin by preparing your ingredients for roasting. Remove the tomatillos' papery outer shell and then blanch them by dropping them into boiling water for 1 minute. Drain and shock with cold water. Core the tomatillos, removing the stems, and then cut them in half. Put them, along with the tortilla, onion, plantain, and both chiles, in a roasting pan and toss with olive oil. Roast for 10 to 15 minutes. When it's done, the tortilla should be well browned and the tomatillos, plantain, and onions thoroughly cooked.

Toast the peanuts, almonds, and walnuts on a baking sheet in the oven at the same temperature or in a small cast-iron pan on the stovetop. Remove them from the heat when you start to smell them, before they turn brown. Transfer the nuts to a bowl and use the same method to toast the sesame seeds, cumin seeds, and aniseed. When they're done, grind up all the nuts and seeds in a mortar and pestle along with the salt, cinnamon, cloves, and epazote. Add the oil and mix to make a loose paste.

Put the roasted fruits and vegetables in a food processor along with the spice and nut paste, and the oregano, mint, cilantro, and lettuce leaves. Blend thoroughly before adding the stock. You want it quite smooth, so let the machine do what it does so well.

Taste the sauce while it's still in the food processor and consider how spicy it is. If you want it to have more heat, grind up a few of those reserved seeds in the mortar and add them to the sauce. Blend, and blend again. Taste. You get the idea. Remember, mole doesn't need to be super spicy and, in fact, super spicy might get in the way of its complex flavors. Still, it should have a solid, if sneaky, heat.

1 teaspoon kosher salt

$1/4$ teaspoon cinnamon

Pinch of ground cloves

$1/2$ teaspoon epazote

1 tablespoon olive oil

2 tablespoons chopped oregano

$1/4$ cup chopped mint

$1/4$ cup chopped cilantro, plus more for garnish

2 lettuce leaves

1 cup chicken stock (page 26)

Finally, transfer the sauce to a pan and gently heat for 20 minutes as the sauce mellows and reduces slightly while you cook your steaks. **To grill,** your coals should be so hot that you can comfortably keep your hand 2 inches above the grate for 3 seconds—just! (For gas grills, this means 450°F.) Put the oiled steak on the hottest part of the grill and sear for 3 to 5 minutes on each side; flank steak cooks quickly, so it might be done at this point. If it needs a bit more time, move it over lower heat and cook for at most 2 to 5 minutes more— it should always be rare! **To pan-fry,** heat the peanut oil in a heavy pan until it's very hot—almost smoking. Sear the steak for 3 minutes on each side over high heat before turning down the burner. Flank steak doesn't take long and that should be all the time the steak needs. If it needs a bit more time, cook over moderate heat for at most 2 to 5 more minutes.

However you cook your steak, check for doneness often, using the finger-poke or the nick-and-peek method (see page 19). Let the steak rest in a warming oven (170°F) or on a warm plate under a loose tent of foil for 5 minutes. Before serving, give it a final dose of salt and a grind of fresh black pepper.

To serve, slice the steak across the grain, creating short slices. I like to spoon the mole sauce under the steak, which lets the top of the steak remain crispy. Add a scoop of the Baked Tortillas to the warm plates and garnish all of it with coarsely chopped cilantro leaves.

Baked Tortillas

3 cups chopped tomato

2 Cubanelle peppers or another mildly spicy pepper, seeded and chopped (2 tablespoons)

1 tablespoon olive oil

6 (6-inch diameter) corn tortillas

2 ounces fresh goat cheese, crumbled

1 teaspoon kosher salt

Preheat the oven to 350°F. In a mixing bowl, toss together the tomatoes, peppers, and olive oil. Stack the tortillas and cut them into quarters. Lay the tortilla pieces out in a baking dish (an 11 by 7-inch oval works great) to form a single layer. Put half the tomato-pepper mixture on top, along with half the cheese and half the salt. Repeat for the second layer, using all the remaining ingredients. Bake for 30 to 40 minutes, or until the cheese begins to brown.

Skirt Steak with Tomatillo Relish,
Avocado Salad, and Yuca in Tangelo Sauce

Tomatillos are easy to walk past in the produce aisle. Because of their papery calyx, most people have no idea what to do with them. Try them once and you'll be hooked. This relish is a great place to start. It puts the tomatillo's bright, lemony flavor to work as a complement to skirt steak. Choose firm fruits still in their husk. As ugly as the tomatillo is pretty, yuca is a staple of the tropics that most Anglos just don't go near. Venture forth. It makes a terrific side dish for Latin-inspired meals. Best of all, you won't have to wonder for another day what that giant brown tuber is doing in your grocery store.

Serves 4

GRILL OR PAN-FRY

2 pounds skirt steak

1 teaspoon kosher salt

Olive oil for rubbing

1 to 2 tablespoons peanut oil for pan-frying

Freshly ground black pepper

TOMATILLO RELISH

4 tomatillos (about the size of a kiwi)

1 serrano chile

3 scallions, sliced into thin rounds

1 clove garlic, minced

Juice of 1/2 lime (about 2 tablespoons)

2 radishes, sliced and coarsely chopped

1/4 cup cilantro, coarsely chopped

1 teaspoon salt

Prepare the steak by salting it, and then let it come to room temperature. Rub with a bit of olive oil just before cooking.

To prepare the tomatillos, peel away the papery husks and then drop them into a pot of boiling water for 3 minutes. This brings out their flavor and softens them. After cooking, rinse with cold water and set to cool on the counter as you prepare everything else. All the ingredients go in one bowl. Scorch the chile by setting it directly over the flame of a gas stove or, if you don't have a flame, pop it in the boiling water with the tomatillos for the final minute. The heat makes it possible to remove the seeds and peel off the skin before chopping it. When the tomatillos are cool, core them as you would a normal tomato and chop, using the whole fruit. Toss with the remaining ingredients and you're done.

To grill, your coals should be so hot that you can comfortably keep your hand 2 inches above the grate for 3 seconds—just! (For gas grills, this means 450°F.) Put the oiled steak on the hottest part of the grill and sear for 3 to 5 minutes on each side over intense heat. Skirt steak cooks quickly, so it might be done; if it needs a bit more time, move it over lower heat and cook at most 2 to 5 minutes more—it should always be rare! **To pan-fry,** heat the peanut oil in a heavy pan until it's very hot—almost smoking. Sear the steak for 3 minutes on each side over high heat before lowering the burner. Skirt steak should be done. If your steak needs a bit more time, cook over moderate heat for at most 2 to 5 minutes more.

However you cook your steak, check for doneness often, using the finger-poke or the nick-and-peek method (see page 19). Generously salt and pepper the steak before resting it in a warming oven (170°F) or on a warm plate under a loose tent of foil for 5 minutes.

Slice the steak lengthwise, creating long, thin strips. Distribute the steak on warm plates, along with equal portions of Avocado Salad and Tomatillo Relish on each side of the steak. A scoop of yuca finishes the plate.

Avocado Salad

Use unblemished Hass avocados. When an avocado begins to discolor on the inside, it affects the taste of the whole fruit. A squeeze of lime, salt, and some crushed, freshly toasted cumin bring out the essence of the fruit.

3 Hass avocados

Juice of 1 lime (2 tablespoons)

1 tablespoon whole cumin, toasted

1 teaspoon kosher salt

Cut the avocados in half. Cut the flesh into cubes by cutting it lengthwise and then across. Run your fingers down the skin on the inside to remove the cubes. Put the avocado cubes in a mixing bowl and immediately squeeze on the lime juice. Toss, and then sprinkle on the cumin and salt. Serve at room temperature.

Yuca in Tangelo Sauce

Juice and zest of 2 tangelos
(^{1}/2 cup juice, 1 teaspoon zest;
substitute tangerines or
Valencia oranges)

1 yuca (about 1 pound)

2 tablespoons olive oil

2 cloves garlic, thinly sliced

1 shallot, chopped

1 teaspoon kosher salt

Freshly ground black pepper

Using a little mild dish soap, wash the tangelos, rinsing carefully. Using a fine grater, zest the cleaned tangelos before juicing. Set aside the zest and juice.

Choose a yuca root that is firm and mold-free—the mold can be difficult to see. Using a big sharp knife and a good dose of caution, cut away the brown skin down to the cream-colored flesh. Once it's peeled, cut the root into 4-inch sections. Take each of those round sections and cut them lengthwise into quarters. You'll find a fibrous strand running down the center, which you should cut away. This can be difficult. If you miss any of it you can remove it after cooking when it will show itself, looking almost like a piece of twine.

Put the yuca in a saucepan and cover with water. Boil, over medium heat, for 30 minutes. Drain and set aside to cool. Once it is cool, prepare the yuca by cutting each of the 4-inch sections across into ^{1}/2-inch slices. Before putting it back into the saucepan, heat the olive oil in the pan and sauté the garlic and shallot over low heat until soft but not colored. Add the yuca, fresh juice, ^{1}/2 teaspoon of the zest, and the salt to the pan with the garlic and shallot. Cook gently for 5 minutes to reduce slightly. Before serving, sprinkle with the remaining ^{1}/2 teaspoon of zest and a grind of black pepper. Taste for salt.

Hangar Steak
with Mango–Cherry Tomato Salsa and Corn Pudding

When tossed with tomatoes, a little scallion, and some hot pepper and coriander, mangoes make a refreshing and complex salsa that I love to eat with a rich steak like hangar. With Corn Pudding, this is a beautiful and easy plate.

Serves 4

GRILL OR PAN-FRY

2 pounds hangar steak

1 teaspoon kosher salt

Olive oil for rubbing

1 to 2 tablespoons peanut oil for pan-frying

Freshly ground black pepper

Prepare the steak by removing the line of gristle down its center (see page 56). It's even easier to ask your butcher to do it for you. Salt the steak and let it come to room temperature. Rub the steak with olive oil before cooking.

To grill, your coals should be so hot that you can comfortably keep your hand 2 inches above the grate for 3 seconds—just! (For gas grills, this means 450°F.) Put the oiled steak on the hottest part of the grill and sear for 3 to 5 minutes on each side over high heat before you begin to fuss over it. That means moving the steak to a cooler part of the grill and cooking for an additional 10 to 14 minutes over moderate heat, flipping, poking, and watching as you work toward crispy-brown perfection. **To pan-fry,** heat the peanut oil in a heavy pan until it's very hot—almost smoking. Sear the steak for 3 minutes on each side over high heat before turning down the burner. Cook over moderate heat for an additional 10 to 14 minutes, turning the steak every few minutes as it slowly browns. If smoke is a problem, put the steak, pan and all, in a 400°F oven to finish cooking.

However you cook your steak, check for doneness often, using the finger-poke method, an instant-read thermometer (120° to 130°F for rare to medium-rare), or the nick-and-peek method (see page 19). Generously salt and pepper the steak before resting it in a warming oven (170°F) or on a warm plate under a loose tent of foil for 5 minutes.

After the meat has rested, slice it into round medallions, distributing them evenly among 4 plates. Add a scoop of Corn Pudding to each plate, a dose of kosher salt and freshly ground pepper, and a scattering of the salsa.

Mango–Cherry Tomato Salsa

To work *with* the steak, rather than alongside it, cut the tomatoes and mangoes into a fine dice.

10 coriander seeds, crushed

Pinch of hot pepper flakes, crushed

2 dozen cherry tomatoes, finely diced (the bright orange Sungold are my favorite)

2 mangoes, peeled and finely diced

5 scallions, ends trimmed, white with some green stem sliced into rounds

1/2 teaspoon kosher salt

Using a mortar and pestle, crush the coriander and red pepper flakes. In a medium bowl, combine the tomatoes, mangoes, and scallions; then add the crushed coriander and pepper flakes and the salt. Stir to combine.

Corn Pudding

1 tablespoon butter

4 ears corn, kernels shaved off the cob (3 cups kernels)

1/2 red bell pepper, or 3 cherry peppers, seeded and diced

2 eggs

1 cup heavy cream

1/2 teaspoon kosher salt

1/4 teaspoon cayenne pepper

Freshly ground black pepper

Preheat the oven to 350°F.

Butter an 8 by 8-inch square pan. Put the corn kernels in the buttered pan and lay the pepper on top. In a small bowl, beat together the eggs, heavy cream, salt, and cayenne pepper and pour it into the pan with the corn and peppers. Bake for 40 minutes, or until firm and just browning on top. Finish with a grind of black pepper.

Dallas Fajitas:

Spicy Skirt Steak, Guacamole, Roasted Sweet Peppers, Black Beans, Corn Salsa, Lettuce, Scallions, Hot Peppers, and Cheese

These fajitas are named after the 1980s Aaron Spelling hit, a TV show that helped define the decade's spirit of ridiculous excess. So what's all that got to do with a fajita? Both, while contributing little to the culture—culinary or otherwise—are irresistible, over-the-top, and hard to get enough of. Pile these up high and eat while watching E! Don't overlook the Guacamole, Roasted Sweet Peppers (page 126), Black Beans (page 135), and Corn Salsa (page 144).

Serves 4

GRILL OR PAN-FRY

1½ pounds skirt steak (substitute flank or top sirloin if you must)

1 teaspoon kosher salt

Olive oil for rubbing

1 to 2 tablespoons peanut oil for pan-frying

Freshly ground black pepper

6 large 8-inch flour tortillas or 10 small 6-inch flour tortillas

2 cups shredded lettuce or baby lettuces

Sour cream (full fat!)

Cilantro, chopped

1 cup grated sharp Cheddar cheese

6 scallions, white and tender green parts, sliced into rounds

Hot sauce (Lottie's, Marie Sharp's, or your favorite)

Chopped chile pepper, seeded (jalapeño or serrano will work)

Prepare the meat by salting it, then let it come to room temperature. Just before cooking, rub with olive oil.

Preheat the oven to 350°F. Wrap the tortillas tightly in foil and put them in the oven to warm up while you get everything ready. For fajitas, all the fixings should be set out on the table so people can make their own the way they like it. Make things pretty by choosing nice bowls to put out the lettuce, sour cream, cilantro, cheese, and scallions. Either hot sauce or chopped chile pepper is essential (or put out both!).

To grill, your coals should be so hot that you can comfortably keep your hand 2 inches above the grate for 3 seconds—just! (For gas grills, this means 450°F.) Put the oiled steak on the hottest part of the grill and sear for 3 to 5 minutes on each side. If your fire is truly hot, that should be all the cooking it needs; if it needs a bit more, move the steak over lower heat and cook for at most 2 to 5 minutes more—skirt steak should always be rare! **To pan-fry,** heat the peanut oil in a heavy pan until it's very hot—almost smoking. Sear the steak for 3 minutes on each side over high heat. Skirt steak should be done at this point. If your steak needs a bit more time, cook over moderate heat for at most 2 to 5 more minutes, turning the steak often as it browns.

However you cook your steak, check for doneness often, using the finger-poke or the nick-and-peek method (see page 19). Generously salt and pepper each steak before resting in a warming oven (170°F) or on a warm plate under a loose tent of foil for 5 minutes.

After resting, slice the steak against the grain, creating long, thin strips, and put them on a warm platter. Take the warm tortillas from the oven and wrap them in a clean napkin or dish towel. Bring the Guacamole to the table along with the Roasted Sweet Peppers, Black Beans, Corn Salsa, and all the other fixings.

Guacamole

Double the recipe if you want to put some of it out with a big bowl of salty corn chips.

1/2 teaspoon cumin seeds, toasted

1 tablespoon minced fresh garlic

1/2 teaspoon kosher salt

1 tablespoon minced jalapeño

2 tablespoons lime juice

3 large avocados, peeled and pitted

10 cherry tomatoes, coarsely chopped

5 scallions, chopped

1/4 cup chopped cilantro

With a mortar and pestle, grind the cumin seeds. Add the garlic, salt, jalapeño, and lime juice and work briefly to blend. Chop the avocado and put it in the mortar with the tomatoes, scallions, and cilantro. Mash briefly. I like my guacamole chunky, not smooth.

CHAPTER FOUR

Far East Steak

This chapter encompasses the cuisines of Thailand, Vietnam, Cambodia, Myanmar (Burma), and Vietnam with major influences from China to the north and India to the west. Add Korea and you have an ambitious range of flavors.

The steaks here are enlivened by chile peppers, ginger, fish sauce, soy sauce, and lime. They call for a pot of jasmine rice and a glass of icy green tea. Refreshing and bright, this kind of food is forgiving of substitutions and innovations, and I encourage that. An extra splash of fish sauce, some perfect snow peas in June, chile peppers until the edge of reason—everything goes.

Before you get started, stock up on the basics, including a great carbon-steel wok (see the Pantry section at the end of the book for where to get one).

Although the list of required ingredients isn't extensive, they are essential. You'll need: Sriracha (hot chile sauce), nam pla (Thai fish sauce), sambal oelek (chili paste), and a pungent dark soy sauce—I like Pearl River Bridge brand's Mushroom Flavored Superior Dark Soy. I also occasionally call for mirin (Japanese cooking wine), fermented bean paste, galangal (fresh or powdered), dried shrimp, shrimp paste, toasted sesame oil, and tamarind paste. It doesn't cost a lot to stock up on these ingredients and they have a decent shelf life. So if you like this kind of spicy, lively food and want to cook it at home, you'll need to make a trip to an Asian grocery. While you're there, buy some Thai jasmine rice (amazing!), pretty chopsticks, rice crackers, and, of course, fortune cookies. If you don't have an Asian grocery nearby, there are other ways to stock up. See the Pantry section at the end of the book for details.

For fresh ingredients, supermarkets increasingly stock lemongrass, fresh ginger, and cilantro. I frequently call for greens, which you will find in overwhelming variety in Asian markets or in the ubiquitous sidewalk shops in the Asian (usually Chinese, but sometimes Korean) neighborhoods of any big city. Grocery stores are getting better about stocking what were once considered exotic greens. Use what you can find.

Nibbles, Starters, and Sweets

If you're serving Asian-style steak, opening a package of spicy rice crackers and wasabi peas to nibble with a drink before the meal couldn't be simpler. Raw peanuts, quickly pan-fried with soy sauce, hot pepper flakes, a dash of five-spice powder, and a little oil also make a good cocktail-time snack. Whatever I do, I like to stay in the spirit of the region—whether that means kimchee, spicy nuts, or shui mai—the food you set out to snack on sets the tone for the evening.

If you're having guests or just want to extend the meal with a first course because you can, a dish of Mango Salad (page 177) set alongside a simple summer roll (page 166, make it with shrimp instead of steak) is a light first course. Asian Slaw (page 174), although probably too simple to stand on its own as a first course, would work nicely next to some Spicy Sesame Noodles (page 179). Of course, a fragrant soup is a classic way to start a meal—and Asian-style soups are devastatingly good. If you want something easy, I like chicken stock (page 26) made potent with the addition of lots of fresh ginger and served with rice noodles and shredded napa cabbage.

None of the countries represented here are famous for elaborate desserts the way the French or Italians are. But that doesn't mean there aren't great ways to finish a meal. Tropical fruits are an effortless way to go. Cut up a bunch of one perfect fruit—mango, papaya, grapefruit, star fruit, guava, lychee nuts, watermelon, pineapple—and serve it with a few crisp nut cookies on the side. If you're more ambitious, tapioca pudding made with fresh coconut milk and topped with toasted almonds is delicious. Whatever you do, simplicity and the flavors of the region are key.

Drinks

Yes, you can drink wine with Asian food. I do it all the time; many of my favorite wines happen to be the ones that go best with this kind of food. Because the steaks, sides, and sauces in this chapter tend to have more low and high notes—sweet, sour, spicy, salty, bitter—you want a wine that can stand up to the chaos. White wine with steak is okay! Among the best to try are New Zealand Sauvignon Blancs (Spy Valley is terrific), which have enough grapefruit-like acidity to stand on their own. A dry Riesling is also an excellent bet (Bonny Doon makes a good one), because it tends to have a little more residual sugar without being sweet. For the same reason the Riesling works, a German Gewürztraminer pairs nicely with the food from this region because it has a little more sugar, floral notes, and a strong finish.

Beer, of course, is a natural with spicy Asian food. The beers from this region, often light lagers, are perfect matches with these recipes. My favorite import is the Japanese beer Hitachino Nest White Ale. But don't overlook American microbrews, which offer a smart, locally made alternative. I love Hefeweizen with spicy food. It's another German invention—a light, wheat-based beer served with a squeeze of lemon—and is very refreshing. Plenty of American brewers make their own versions.

Wasabi-Stuffed Filet
with Pickled Ginger and Daikon-Watercress Relish

A take on the ginger-wasabi combination that accompanies sushi, this steak is best with a pile of Jasmine Rice with yet more soy-wasabi sauce. The Daikon-Watercress Relish is somewhere between a slaw and a salad. I call it a relish because it rounds out a forkful of the filet and the rice like nothing else can.

Serves 4

GRILL OR PAN-FRY

4 filets (2 inches thick)

1 teaspoon kosher salt

Olive oil for rubbing

6 tablespoons wasabi powder

5 to 6 tablespoons water

1 to 2 tablespoons peanut oil for pan-frying

Freshly ground black pepper

Pickled ginger (sushi ginger)

Soy sauce

Using a paring knife, slice sideways into each steak from a single, small entry point—as if you're opening a hole in a round of pita bread. Gently form a pocket in the center of the steak. Remove the knife and reverse it to cut in both directions, going close to the sides of the steak without cutting through. Use your finger to feel how successful you've been at creating the widest possible pocket.

Salt the steaks and let them come to room temperature. Rub with olive oil just before cooking.

Mix the wasabi and enough water together in a small bowl to form a smooth paste. Use your finger to smear the wasabi paste inside the steak—use about $1^{1}/_{2}$ teaspoons per steak. Reserve the remaining paste.

To grill, your coals should be so hot that you can comfortably keep your hand 2 inches above the grate for 3 seconds—just! (For gas grills, this means 450°F.) Put the oiled steaks on the hottest part of the grill and sear for 3 to 5 minutes on each side over high heat before you begin to fuss over them. That means moving the steaks to a cooler part of the grill and cooking for an additional 6 to 10 minutes over moderate heat, flipping, poking, and watching as you work toward crispy-brown perfection. **To pan-fry,** heat the peanut oil in a heavy pan until it's very hot—almost smoking. Sear the steaks for 3 minutes on each side over high heat before turning down the burner. Cook the steaks over moderate heat for an additional 6 to 10 minutes, turning them every few minutes as they slowly brown. Depending on how thick they are, and how smoky you can stand your kitchen, you may need to put the steaks, pan and all, in a 400°F oven to finish cooking.

However you cook your steaks, check for doneness often, using the finger-poke method, an instant-read thermometer (120° to 130°F for rare to medium-rare), or the nick-and-peek method (see page 19). Generously salt and pepper each steak before resting in a warming oven (170°F) or on a warm plate under a loose tent of foil to rest for 5 minutes.

Before serving, smear a thin coating of wasabi paste on the top of each steak and then artfully pile 3 or 4 slices of ginger in the center of each steak. Add a portion of the relish to the plate, a generous pile of rice and, to finish, place a disk of wasabi paste next to a pile of ginger on each plate. Put a pitcher of soy sauce on the table, and, if you have them, small bowls or saucers so people can mix their own wasabi and soy at the table.

Daikon-Watercress Relish

1 large daikon radish, in strips, or 1 large bunch Cheery Belle red radishes, shredded

1 cup watercress, stemmed

1 teaspoon rice vinegar

1/2 teaspoon kosher salt

Use a julienne peeler or a regular vegetable peeler to cut long pieces of the daikon. Depending on the peeler you use, you'll end up with long spaghetti-like strips or with thin peelings. Either kind works. Toss the daikon shreds with the watercress leaves, vinegar, and salt in a mixing bowl.

Jasmine Rice

Fresh and fragrant, the best rice comes from Thailand and arrives with a date on the bag.

2 cups jasmine rice

3 1/2 cups water

1 teaspoon kosher salt

Combine all the ingredients in a pot over medium heat, cover, and cook until all the water has been absorbed and the rice is tender but not mushy. This takes 15 minutes or so. Fluff gently with a fork before serving.

Lime–Chile Sauce Marinated Skirt Steak Wraps:
Peanuts, Vermicelli Noodles, and Shredded Carrots with Mung Bean Salad

Some days, it's so hot out that eating hot food is impossible. When that happens—usually in late August, and the humidity is hovering around 95 percent—a cool summer roll, with its combination of mint, salty peanuts, spicy sauce, and rice noodles, is just what I want. Using steak rather than shrimp makes these rolls more like dinner than a snack by giving them some heft. Serve with Mung Bean Salad and Jasmine Rice (page 165), if you think you need it. Ice down some Tsingtao beer to serve alongside.

Serves 4

GRILL OR PAN-FRY

3 tablespoons lime juice

1 tablespoon olive oil

3 tablespoons sambal oelek (chili paste)

1 teaspoon kosher salt

2 pounds skirt steak

1 to 2 tablespoons peanut oil for pan-frying

SWEET CHILI SAUCE

3 tablespoons hoisin sauce

1 tablespoon fish sauce

1 tablespoon rice vinegar

1 teaspoon sambal oelek (chili paste)

2 tablespoons finely chopped peanuts

3 ounces vermicelli rice noodles (rice sticks)

20 summer roll wraps

2 cups shredded carrots

2/3 cup chopped mint

1/3 cup chopped basil (Thai basil is great, too)

2/3 cup coarsely chopped peanuts

Combine the lime juice, olive oil, chili paste, and salt in a glass or other nonreactive baking dish. Add the steak and marinate for 1 hour on the counter or for up to 24 hours refrigerated. Rub the steak with some additional olive oil just before cooking.

To make the Sweet Chili Sauce, combine the hoisin, fish sauce, vinegar, chili paste, and finely chopped peanuts together in a small pot over low heat. Simmer the sauce for 3 minutes.

Soak the noodles for 15 to 20 minutes in cold water. Drain and set aside.

To grill, your coals should be so hot that you can comfortably keep your hand 2 inches above the grate for 3 seconds—just! (For gas grills, this means 450°F.) Put the oiled steak on the hottest part of the grill and sear for 3 minutes on each side. This should make for crispy-brown steak. If your steak needs a bit more time, move it to a cooler part of the grill and cook over moderate heat for at most 2 to 5 more minutes.

To pan-fry, heat the peanut oil in a heavy pan until it's very hot—almost smoking. Sear the steak for 3 minutes on each side over high heat. If your steak needs a bit more time, turn down the burner and cook over moderate heat for at most 2 to 5 minutes more.

However you cook your steak, check for doneness often, using the finger-poke or the nick-and-peek method (see page 19). Transfer the steak to a cool plate and rest it for 10 minutes, uncovered. You want it to cool off without getting cold.

When it's no longer hot, but still above room temperature, slice the steak into short, thin pieces. For flank steak you need to cut against the grain of the meat—across, not along, the length of the steak.

Prepare the summer roll wraps by submerging them in warm water for 2 to 3 minutes. To see whether they're ready, peel some of them apart—you'll be able to tell whether they've absorbed enough water to be pliable and tender. Once they're tender, drain the warm water and replace it with a little cool water—just enough to keep the wraps moist as you work. Set aside until you're ready to use them. (Some wrappers will rip; don't worry, I've called for extra.)

Lay out a wrapper on a clean surface, add a slice or two of meat, some shredded carrot, mint, noodles, basil, and coarsely chopped peanuts. The recipe makes between 14 and 16 summer rolls. Spoon about a teaspoon of sauce down the length of each one before wrapping it up as you would a burrito. These work best if you don't overfill them; keep the filling in a line down the center, but don't fill all the way to the end. That way, when you pick it up to eat it, the filling will stay inside. Put the rolls on a cold platter and refrigerate briefly before serving with the Mung Bean Salad.

Mung Bean Salad

5 cups water

1 cup whole mung beans, with the green shell on

2 whole Thai peppers

1 teaspoon salt

2 teaspoons sambal oelek

1 teaspoon fish sauce

8 scallions, white with some green, chopped

1/2 cup finely shredded unsweetened coconut, toasted

In a saucepan, combine the water, mung beans, and Thai peppers and cook over medium heat for 35 minutes. Taste the beans for tenderness. Don't let the pot go dry, but try to allow the beans to absorb all the water by the time they are cooked. If necessary, add small amounts of water until the beans are tender.

Let the beans cool a bit and then fish out the peppers. Mince them before returning them to the pot, along with the salt, sambal oelek, fish sauce, scallions, and coconut. Refrigerate and serve cold.

Thin-Sliced Sirloin
over Rainbow Swiss Chard with Hot Mustard

Forget about exotic ingredients or a complex marinade—this is an easy, fast recipe that puts steak to work with stunning rainbow chard. Serve with Jasmine Rice (page 165).

Serves 4

WOK

1¹/₂ pounds sirloin steak (or substitute flank steak or skirt steak)

HOT MUSTARD MARINADE

2 tablespoons dark soy sauce (mushroom soy is my favorite)

1 tablespoon mustard seeds

1 tablespoon peanut oil

1 tablespoon dry mustard

1 large bunch rainbow Swiss chard, coarsely chopped (about 5 to 6 cups)

2 tablespoons peanut oil

3 cloves garlic, peeled and crushed with the side of a knife

2 tablespoons grated fresh ginger

1 tablespoon dark soy sauce

1 tablespoon mirin (Japanese cooking wine)

2 teaspoons cornstarch dissolved in 1 tablespoon water

¹/₂ cup chicken stock or water

Sriracha sauce (optional)

MUSTARD SAUCE

3 tablespoons Chinese hot mustard or 2 tablespoons dry Chinese mustard

1 teaspoon peanut oil

¹/₂ to 1 teaspoon water

Trim off any excess visible fat from the rim of the steak before cutting into thin, 2- to 3-inch-long strips. Whisk together the soy sauce, mustard seeds, 1 tablespoon of the peanut oil, and dry mustard in the flat dish you plan to use to marinate your steak. Add the strips of meat and let it stand on the counter for up to an hour or refrigerate for up to 24 hours.

Trim the rough stem ends of the Swiss chard, rinse, and discard any ragged or discolored leaves. Lay the Swiss chard on the counter with the stems together like a bouquet of flowers and cut from the stem end up, creating ¹/₂-inch pieces. Continue up to the leaves, giving them an extra chop if they're very large. Make one pile of chopped leaves and one pile of stems.

To cook the chard, heat your wok over the hottest burner on high. When the wok itself is hot, add 1 tablespoon of the oil. When the oil is hot, add the garlic, ginger, and the stems of the Swiss chard. Toss to coat with oil and cook for 3 to 5 minutes. Add the leaves and cook for 1 to 2 minutes longer, until the leaves have wilted. Add the soy sauce, mirin, and cornstarch mixture along with ¹/₄ cup of the stock. Let the greens cook for 5 minutes or so, tossing and stirring constantly and adding more stock if the wok gets dry or starts to smoke. Taste for seasoning and add more soy sauce or a squirt of Sriracha if you want the greens to be spicy. Transfer the greens to a serving bowl, cover with foil, and place the bowl in a warming oven (170°F) until ready to serve.

Remove the meat from the marinade. To cook the steak, heat the wok and add the remaining tablespoon of peanut oil. Allow it to become *very* hot before adding half the meat (maybe even one-third depending on how big your wok is). You want the beef to get crispy—if your burner isn't very strong or there's too much meat in the wok at one time you'll end up with (ugh) steamed meat. Avoid this by working slowly and tossing the meat up the sides of the wok to separate it. Keep that burner on high. The meat will cook quickly, so take it out as soon as it browns. Set each batch aside, uncovered, in the warming oven (170°F).

If you have a bottle of Chinese hot mustard, use that. If not, make your own mustard sauce by combining the dry mustard with the oil and just enough water to make a soft paste. Serve in layers starting with the jasmine rice next to the greens with the crispy bits of steak on top. A dab of the hot mustard rounds it out. Chopsticks are a must.

Li Hung Chang's Chop Suey
with Flat Iron Steak, Bok Choy, Bean Sprouts, and Mushrooms

Li Hung Chang was a Chinese diplomat who arrived in New York late in the summer of 1896. At a banquet held in his honor at the Waldorf, the *New York Times* reported that his companions "ate fish, flesh and fowl, drank several kinds of wine, and finished with coffee" while Chang ate nearly nothing. After making a "last effort to eat American food," his attendant brought him chopped chicken, vegetable soup, and rice—a combination that is generically referred to today, and at Chinese restaurants across the country, as chop suey. This he ate happily, in a flash of ivory chopsticks. Whether or not chop suey is named after Chang's meal that night, the dish chop suey is worth reclaiming from dreary Chinese menus from Arizona to Maine. By making it the right way—no canned water chestnuts, frozen peas, or MSG necessary—this is a fresh, unassuming meal. It's what you wish came out of your little white carton of Chinese takeout, but rarely does. Serve with Jasmine Rice (page 165).

Serves 4

WOK

MARINADE

2 tablespoons Sriracha sauce (substitute chiles if you prefer)

1 tablespoon mirin (Japanese cooking wine)

1 tablespoon cornstarch dissolved in water

1 tablespoon mushroom soy sauce or dark soy sauce

3 cloves garlic, minced

1 finger fresh ginger, peeled and chopped (2 to 3 tablespoons)

1 tablespoon fermented bean paste

1 pound flat iron steak (also called top blade), flank steak, or skirt steak

3 tablespoons peanut oil

1 sweet yellow onion, sliced

1 head broccoli, cut or broken into small florets

In a shallow dish, combine the Sriracha, mirin, cornstarch, soy sauce, garlic, ginger, and bean paste. Slice the steak very thin (about 1/4 inch) across the grain. Put the beef into the dish and toss to coat. Marinate on the counter for 1 hour or up to 24 hours in the refrigerator.

Get your wok smoking hot, add 2 tablespoons of the peanut oil, and heat until it's glistening. Using your hands or a slotted spoon, remove the beef from the marinade and put it all into the hot oil (save the marinade—you'll be using it later). Go fast and hot—you want to sear the beef without letting it get tough. Using a wooden spoon, move the pieces up the sides of the wok, tossing and spreading as you go. It shouldn't take more than about 3 minutes. Don't overcook it. If you still see some pink on the edges, that's okay. Rest the steak in a warming oven (170°F) or on a warm plate under a loose tent of foil for 5 minutes.

To cook the vegetables, add the remaining 1 tablespoon (or just another splash) of peanut oil, let it heat, and then add the onion, broccoli, pepper, and mushrooms. Using a rubber spatula, get every last bit of the marinade out of the dish and into the wok and add the cornstarch. Stir and let it get hot. When it's simmering, add the chicken stock and bok choy and toss to combine. Keep it moving over your highest heat and when the bok choy is tender and all the vegetables are softened but still crisp, toss in the cooked meat and the bean

1 red, orange, or yellow pepper, chopped

10 shiitake mushrooms or 1¹/₂ cups trimmed and sliced mushrooms (any mushrooms will do)

2 teaspoons cornstarch dissolved in a little stock

¹/₂ cup chicken stock (page 26)

2 small heads bok choy, sliced lengthwise

¹/₂ cup bean sprouts

sprouts. All you're doing is reheating the meat and coating the whole mixture with what should be a glistening brown sauce.

Remove from the heat and serve over rice, distributing the fragrant sauce from the bottom of the wok evenly over each dish. Chopsticks and a cold beer complete it.

Crispy Beef Satay
with Spicy Peanut Dipping Sauce and Asian Slaw

Peanuts and meat are a winning combination. Just ask Elvis. If he was a little too into the bliss of the bacon-peanut combo before Thai food caught on in this country, it's hard to blame him. A bit of spice gives this dish depth. Pile up these bamboo skewers on a platter, toss together some Asian Slaw, and be sure to make a big, steaming bowl of fragrant Jasmine Rice (page 165).

Serves 4

GRILL

2 pounds skirt steak, sirloin, hangar, or top blade steak

3 good-size cloves garlic, minced (3 tablespoons)

3 bird chiles (Thai chiles) or other small chiles, seeded and chopped (about 1 tablespoon)

2 shallots, diced (2 to 3 tablespoons)

2 tablespoons Thai fish sauce

2 tablespoons brown sugar

Juice of 1 lime (about 2 tablespoons)

1 tablespoon peanut oil

SPICY PEANUT DIPPING SAUCE

1 cup unsweetened coconut milk

$1/2$ cup smooth peanut butter

1 tablespoon brown sugar

2 tablespoons Thai fish sauce

$1/3$ cup warm water

2 tablespoons lime juice (about 1 lime)

1 tablespoon Thai chili garlic sauce

$1/2$ teaspoon galangal powder or 1 tablespoon grated fresh galangal (optional)

2 tablespoons Thai green curry paste (mae ploy)

I've tried grilling many kinds of meat for this recipe. Skirt steak is hard to beat. Slice the meat $1/2$ inch thick across the grain, and then cut those long slices into pieces 3 inches long. Combine the garlic, chiles, shallots, fish sauce, brown sugar, and lime juice in a shallow dish, add the meat, and toss to combine. Let sit on the counter for 1 hour or in the refrigerator for up to 24 hours. Soak a dozen bamboo skewers in enough water to cover.

To make the dipping sauce, whisk all the ingredients together in a pot. Cook over low heat, whisking often, for 15 to 20 minutes. The mixture should be thick and velvety, not gummy. The consistency of peanut butter varies, so add a bit more water or cook to reduce as needed. Remove from the heat, transfer to a small bowl, and allow to stand at room temperature.

Drain the marinade and drizzle the meat with the oil. Once it's more oily than wet, begin threading it onto the presoaked bamboo skewers, with each piece poked twice or three times through lengthwise. It's important to cook the skewers over nice hot coals—you should be able to hold your hand 2 inches above the grate for 3 seconds, but not much longer. Cooking the thin meat on the skewers will take around 3 minutes per side. Don't crowd the meat or it won't brown evenly. A little char is essential. Be sure to rest the skewers in a warming oven (170°F) for 5 minutes after cooking, as you would any steak.

Serve on a platter with the dipping sauce, and bring a bowl of Asian Slaw to the table. I like to let people grab their own skewers and reach for a couple of common bowls of peanut sauce. Getting your hands dirty adds to the pleasant buzz of a good meal.

Asian Slaw

Sweet, tangy, and a just a little bit spicy, this slaw can be eaten alongside any of the Asian-inspired dishes in this chapter. No need to peel European cucumbers—they're the really long ones that usually come wrapped in plastic in the produce section. Other varieties of cucumber, with bitter or tough skin, should be peeled.

1/2 head Savoy cabbage (other varieties will do)

1/2 cucumber, European if possible

3 tablespoons rice vinegar

1/2 teaspoon toasted sesame oil

2 teaspoons sweet chili sauce (such as mae ploy)

1 teaspoon olive oil

1 tablespoon black sesame seeds

Kosher salt

Sriracha sauce (optional)

Cut the cabbage into chunks and shred with a food processor or chop. Using a vegetable peeler, make long threads out of the cucumber and combine them with the cabbage. Beat together the vinegar, sesame oil, chili sauce, olive oil, and sesame seeds. Toss the dressing with the cabbage and cucumbers and add salt to taste. If you want it spicier, add a squirt of Sriracha.

Tamarind-Marinated Flank Steak
with Coconut Rice and Mango Salad

Tamarind, a pulpy, odd-looking fruit most often used to flavor fizzy drinks, has a potent punch of acidity and a toasted sweetness that's delicious in a range of foods. This marinade will tenderize your flank steak while imparting a nicely tropical note. Pair it with Coconut Rice and Mango Salad. A little tamarind paste whisked into some seltzer and rum might inspire, too.

Serves 4

GRILL OR PAN-FRY

2 pounds flank steak, sirloin, skirt steak, or top blade steak

3 tablespoons olive oil, plus more for rubbing

1 onion, coarsely chopped (about 1 cup)

3 cloves garlic, sliced

1 tablespoon whole mustard seeds

$1/2$ cup rice wine vinegar

$1/4$ cup dark molasses

2 tablespoons tamarind paste

1 tablespoon black peppercorns

1 tablespoon whole coriander seed

$1/2$ teaspoon cardamom seed

1 to 2 tablespoons peanut oil for pan-frying

Kosher salt and freshly ground black pepper

Place the steak in a shallow dish.

Heat the olive oil in a pan and sauté the onion over low heat until soft, 10 to 15 minutes. Add the garlic and mustard seeds, stirring until the mustard seeds pop. Add the vinegar, molasses, tamarind paste, peppercorns, coriander, and cardamom. Continue to cook until the mixture reduces enough that you can scoot it to one side of the frying pan without having it spread out. Remove from the heat, allow to cool, and spoon it over the meat, coating both sides generously. Marinate for 1 hour on the counter or up to 24 in the refrigerator.

After the steak has marinated, scrape away any large bits of marinade and then rub with olive oil. **To grill,** your coals should be so hot that you can comfortably keep your hand 2 inches above the grate for 3 seconds—just! (For gas grills, this means 450°F.) Put the oiled steak on the hottest part of the grill and sear for 3 to 5 minutes on each side. That should be all the cooking flank steak needs; don't overcook it. If it needs a bit more time, move it over lower heat and cook for at most 2 to 5 minutes more—it should always be rare! **To pan-fry,** heat the peanut oil in a heavy pan until it's very hot—almost smoking. Sear the steak for 3 minutes on each side over high heat. That should do it for a flank steak. If your steak needs a bit more time, turn down the burner and cook over moderate heat for at most 2 to 5 more minutes.

However you cook your steak, check for doneness often, using the finger-poke or the nick-and-peek method (see page 19). Generously salt and pepper each steak before resting in a warming oven (170°F) or on a warm plate under a loose tent of foil for 5 minutes.

Slice the steak across the grain (making short pieces, not long ones as you do with skirt steak). Serve on a big platter with the Coconut Rice. Pass the bowl of Mango Salad at the table.

Coconut Rice

Make this an opportunity to whack open a fresh coconut. The water you get from the flesh of the fresh nut is nothing like the canned coconut "milk" you buy at the store.

1 young coconut, or $1/2$ cup coconut water and 1 cup freshly grated coconut, plus more for garnish

1 cup boiling water

1 $1/2$ cups jasmine rice

1 teaspoon kosher salt

To collect the coconut water *and* make your own milk, puncture the top of the coconut and drain the water into a glass. This process usually yields about $1/2$ cup of coconut water. Set the water aside. Next, crack open the coconut and remove the flesh from the hard shell. Grate the meat and measure out 1 cup plus a little more for garnish. Transfer the 1 cup grated coconut to a bowl, and cover with the boiling water. Let the mixture sit for 1 hour before straining the water into a cup with the fresh coconut water, reserving the grated coconut. Add plain water to the mixture for a total of $2^1/2$ cups of liquid. Combine the rice, coconut liquid, salt, and $1/4$ cup of the reserved grated coconut in a saucepan with a lid. Cook, covered, for 12 to 15 minutes, or until the liquid has evaporated and the rice is tender. Garnish with a fine grating of coconut.

Mango Salad

This salad is pungent stuff. If you make it with juicy, sweet, super-ripe mangoes, it'll be more like soup when makes it to the table. Made with the firm fruit, it is more deserving of its name. I find it irresistable either way.

2 mangoes

2 tablespoons lime juice

2 teaspoons Sriracha sauce

$1/3$ cup chopped dried shrimp or 1 tablespoon shrimp paste (See Pantry section)

3 tablespoons chopped peanuts

2 tablespoons pomegranate juice

2 tablespoons Thai fish sauce (nam pla)

1 or 2 shallots, chopped (2 tablespoons)

2 tablespoons minced fresh galangal or fresh ginger

Begin by slicing each mango down its length on both sides. If you have a very ripe fruit, the peel will come away easily and you can slice the flesh off the pit and then dice it. For less ripe fruit, it's easier to cut as close to the pit as possible on each side, then work each side away from the pit. Once the mango is in separate halves, cut the fruit, still in the peel, in a criss-cross pattern. Remove it from the peel by bending the peel backward, against its natural curve, to expose the cubes. Combine with the remaining ingredients in colorful bowl. If you are using dried shrimp, let the salad sit for 15 minutes before serving to give the shrimp a chance to soften.

Flat Iron Steak with Ginger,
Asian Pear, and Savoy Cabbage over Spicy Sesame Noodles

This is an unexpectedly delicious combination: marinated steak along with sweet, crisp Asian pear. All of it matches up nicely with the Spicy Sesame Noodles made from soba noodles. These foreign-looking noodles, which show up so often in Korean food, are worth a trip to the Asian grocery or health food store.

Serves 4
WOK

2 pounds flat iron steak

2 tablespoons dark soy sauce

2 tablespoons rice wine

1 finger ginger, grated (about 3 tablespoons)

2 cloves garlic, crushed

1 tablespoon sesame seeds

3 tablespoons peanut oil

1 Asian pear or just-ripe Anjou or Bosc pear

1/2 lime, juiced (about 1 tablespoon)

2 cups shredded Savoy cabbage or white cabbage

1/4 cup chopped peanuts for garnish

2 scallions, chopped, for garnish

If you've bought a whole flat iron steak you'll need to remove the tendon that goes down the center of the meat and any other tendons that run through the meat (see page 92 for directions). If that's been done for you, you'll be looking at fairly narrow, rectangular steaks. From there, slice the steaks into long, 1-inch-thick strips, working against the grain of the meat.

Combine the soy sauce, rice wine, ginger, garlic, sesame seeds, and 1 tablespoon of the peanut oil in a shallow baking dish. Add the pieces of steak and toss to coat. Let them marinate for 1 hour on the counter or for up to 24 hours in the refrigerator.

When you're ready to cook the meat, heat the wok over your hottest burner turned on high. Before the wok begins to glow, add the remaining 2 tablespoons of peanut oil and let that start to shimmer and move—the metal and oil should be very hot before you add the meat. Watch out for spatters as you put the sliced meat into the oil, leaving behind any extra marinade. Using a wooden spoon, move the meat around and up the sides of the wok. Avoid steaming the meat by keeping it out of the juices in the bottom of the wok; 3 to 5 minutes in a very hot wok should be plenty. You want the meat a little rare and tender, not overcooked. Transfer the meat to a platter, but don't stack it. Put the platter in a warming oven (170°F) to rest for 5 minutes.

While the meat rests, core and dice the Asian pear and toss the pieces in a small bowl with the lime juice. To serve, layer the various ingredients either in individual bowls or on one large platter. Begin with the noodles, then add some of the steak, the Asian pear, and then some of the chopped cabbage on top of that. Finish with the peanuts and scallions.

Spicy Sesame Noodles

2 tablespoons rice vinegar

1 tablespoon soy sauce

1 tablespoon Sriracha sauce

1 or 2 cloves garlic, minced
(about 1 tablespoon)

1 teaspoon raw sugar (see
page 29) or brown sugar

2 tablespoons raw tahini

1 tablespoon raw sesame seeds

1 teaspoon toasted sesame oil

1 teaspoon kosher salt

1 pound soba noodles (wheat-
buckwheat noodles)

5 scallions, ends trimmed,
bottom third chopped

To make the sauce for the noodles, combine the rice vinegar, soy sauce, Sriracha sauce, garlic, sugar, and tahini together in a small saucepan and bring to a boil. Remove from the heat after 1 minute. Toast the sesame seeds in a heavy pan until fragrant and add them to the sauce along with the sesame oil. Stir to combine and set aside.

To cook the noodles, boil a large pot of salted water. When you have a rolling boil, add the noodles and cook according to thickness (the package should guide you; if not, test them after 5 minutes). Drain the noodles into a colander, run cold water over them to rinse, drain again, and then while they're still a little warm, combine them with the sauce. Use it all, working the sauce through the noodles. Top with the scallions.

Lemongrass Flank Steak
with Broccoli, Snow Peas, and Lotus Root

This might be my favorite marinade. Fish sauce, such a wonderfully potent liquid, goes amazingly well with beef. Cooked down into a potent syrup, it's even better. Serve with Jasmine Rice (page 165).

Serves 4

WOK

LEMONGRASS MARINADE

2 tablespoons raw sugar (see page 29)

2 tablespoons water

1/4 cup Thai fish sauce

1/2 cup water

4 stalks lemongrass, bottom third peeled and chopped

6 cloves garlic, minced

4 scallions, white parts chopped

1 tablespoon dark soy sauce

1 pound flank steak, skirt steak, sirloin, or top blade steak

2 tablespoons peanut oil

1 teaspoon hot pepper flakes

3 cloves garlic, sliced

1 head broccoli, trimmed into bite-size florets

1 large head or 3 baby heads bok choy, sliced into bite-size pieces (about 2 cups)

1 cup snow peas or green beans

1 lotus root or sun choke, peeled and sliced

2 tablespoons dark soy sauce

1 cup bean sprouts

A squirt of Sriracha sauce

To make the marinade, whisk the sugar and the 2 tablespoons water together in a heavy saucepan over medium heat, stirring until the mixture begins to caramelize. You'll know when it does this because it will start to smell incredible—like caramel corn. Don't burn it—it'll quickly go from fragrant perfection to a scorched disaster. Once you smell it, immediately add the fish sauce and the 1/2 cup water. Whisk the mixture, still cooking it gently, until the sugar is fully dissolved. Add the lemongrass, garlic, scallions, and soy sauce. Give it one last good stir, take it off the heat, and set aside.

Slice the flank steak against the grain into thin slices. The slices can be long, but no piece should be more than 1/4 to 1/2 inch thick. After slicing, spread the meat in a flat dish, pour on the marinade, toss to coat, and let sit for an hour on the counter. Or, if you're working ahead, cover and refrigerate for up to 24 hours.

When you're ready to cook and have all your vegetables ready, heat your wok. Use your hottest burner turned on high. Before the wok begins to glow, add the peanut oil and let that start to shimmer and move—the metal should be very hot. Watch out for spatters as you put in half of the marinated steak. Using a wooden spoon, move it around and up the sides of the wok. Avoid steaming the meat; 3 minutes or so in a very hot wok should be plenty. You're going for crispy but not necessarily cooked through. Transfer the meat to a platter but don't stack it. Put the platter in a warming oven (170°F) to rest for 5 minutes. Save any marinade left in the wok for the vegetables.

Once you finish cooking the meat, the wok should be hot and full of flavorful oil and bits. Add just a little more oil if there isn't a puddle already, heat, then add the pepper flakes, garlic, broccoli, and any other hard vegetables you might have decided to add (carrots, kohlrabi). Toss them around for a few minutes; if it smokes, add a little of the water and any leftover marinade (1/4 cup at most). Next, add the bok choy, snow peas, and lotus root. Toss a bit more before adding the soy sauce. Finally, before the vegetables overcook, add the bean sprouts and toss just long enough to heat them while also coating them with the flavored oil. If the wok dries and begins to smoke, add a little water to keep the vegetables cooking.

Your rice should be cooked and ready. For a casual dinner, I like to pile the vegetables on top of the rice in big, individual bowls and then put the beef on top. To serve a larger group family style, do the same in one large, wide bowl, or use a platter. With some Sriracha hot sauce on the table, people can adjust the heat to their own taste.

Ginger Matchstick, Sweet Pepper, Shiitake Mushroom, and Skirt Steak Wok

Don't be scared by the shocking volume of ginger here. Trust me. As long as you use fresh, unwrinkled ginger—the old stuff is stringy and bitter—you'll welcome these little matchstick-size pieces that blast happily through the more subtle flavors of the meat and vegetables. Because the ginger and beef combination is so central, you can use any vegetables you have on hand. Buy whatever is fresh and in season. Serve with Jasmine Rice (page 165).

Sea beans (Salicornia)—also known as pickle weed, saltwort or, in Europe, samphire—are crisp, branched stalks that thrive in the salty water of oceanside marshes worldwide. If you can find some, they add the salty essence of the sea to your vegetable mix. If you can't, don't worry.

Serves 4

WOK

1 pound skirt steak, flank steak, or top sirloin steak

2 tablespoons Thai fish sauce (nam pla)

2 tablespoons mirin (Japanese rice wine)

2 tablespoons peanut oil

1/2 pound shiitake mushrooms, trimmed and sliced (1 cup)

2 large fingers fresh ginger, peeled and cut into matchsticks (1 cup)

4 cloves garlic, peeled and crushed

1/2 red bell pepper, seeded and sliced into matchstick-size strips

1/2 orange bell pepper, seeded and sliced into matchstick-size strips

2 ounces sea beans or 1 cup broccoli florets

2 tablespoons bean paste

2 to 3 tablespoons Sriracha sauce

1/3 cup coarsely chopped salted peanuts for garnish

1/3 cup cilantro leaves for garnish

Begin by slicing the steak into thin, bite-size strips; keep in mind that they will shrink when they cook. Put the strips of meat in a shallow dish and toss with the fish sauce and rice wine. Cover and let the steak marinate for at least 1 hour on the counter or for up to 24 hours in the refrigerator.

The idea is to make the pieces of vegetables and the meat the same size. This will help everything cook evenly—and it looks pretty on the plate that way. Heat your wok until it's quite hot, and then add the peanut oil. Let the oil get very hot (without smoking) before you add the shiitakes and the ginger. Be careful not to get spattered by hot oil. Let them cook, tossing occasionally, for about 2 minutes. Next add the garlic, bell peppers, and sea beans. Toss and keep the mixture moving for 2 to 3 minutes. Test a piece of ginger for doneness. It should be soft and fairly mellow but not mushy. When your vegetables are ready, stir in the bean paste and toss before transferring to a plate. Keep the heat on the wok high and add the sliced meat and any of the remaining marinade. Toss vigorously for a minute or two. Avoid overcooking the meat. Once the meat has cooked, add the vegetables back into the wok to reheat them while using the wok to mix them with the meat. Taste for seasoning—add a squirt of Sriracha if it's not spicy enough and more fish sauce or soy sauce if it needs salt.

Serve the beef and vegetables mixture on a warm platter, sprinkled with peanuts and cilantro. The Jasmine Rice should be passed separately.

Strip Steak with Pomegranate Reduction,
Saffron Rice, and Gingered Carrots

This is a bright winter-time steak. I love pomegranates, which show up in stores starting in September and disappear sometime in February. Rather than using pomegranate molasses to make the sauce, I like to go straight to the source and reduce pomegranate juice to make a spicy, tart sauce that goes nicely with Saffron Rice (page 190); the Gingered Carrots really complement the exotic flavors here.

Serves 4

GRILL OR PAN-FRY

4 strip steaks

1 teaspoon kosher salt

Olive oil for rubbing

1 to 2 tablespoons peanut oil for pan-frying

POMEGRANATE REDUCTION

1 cup pomegranate juice

3 tablespoons rice vinegar

2 teaspoons hot pepper flakes

$1/2$ teaspoon salt

$1/2$ cup pomegranate kernels, for garnish

2 sprigs cilantro, chopped, for garnish

Prepare the steaks by salting them, and then allow them come to room temperature. Rub them with olive oil just before cooking.

Prepare the reduction a little ahead, so it can cool and thicken. Combine the juice, vinegar, hot pepper flakes, and salt together in a small saucepan and simmer for 25 to 30 minutes. The mixture should reduce to $1/2$ cup and be thick and glossy once it cools.

To grill, your coals should be so hot that you can comfortably hold your hand 2 inches above the grate for 3 seconds—just! (For gas grills, this means 450°F.) Put the oiled steaks on the hottest part of the grill and sear for 3 to 5 minutes on each side over intense heat before you begin to fuss over them. That means moving the steaks to a cooler part of the grill and cooking for an additional 6 to 10 minutes while flipping, poking, and watching as you work toward crispy-brown perfection. **To pan-fry,** heat the peanut oil in a heavy pan until it's very hot—almost smoking. Sear the steaks for 3 minutes on each side over high heat before turning down the burner. Cook an additional 6 to 10 minutes over moderate heat, turning the steaks every few minutes as they slowly brown. If your house is filling with smoke, you can finish the steaks by putting them, pan and all, in a 400°F oven.

However you cook your steaks, check for doneness often, using the finger-poke method, an instant-read thermometer (120° to 130°F for rare to medium-rare), or the nick-and-peek method (see page 19). Rest the steaks for 5 minutes in a warming oven (170°F) or on a warm plate under a loose tent of foil.

To serve, pool some of the reduction on each plate and garnish with the pomegranate kernels and cilantro leaves.

Gingered Carrots

.2 teaspoons peeled and grated fresh ginger

1 teaspoon chopped crystallized ginger

1/2 teaspoon ground ginger

1 teaspoon sugar (raw if you have it)

1 teaspoon kosher salt

2 tablespoons unsalted butter or olive oil

2 tablespoons water

6 good-size carrots, peeled and cut in half lengthwise and then in half again

Put all the ingredients in a heavy pot and cover. Cook over very low heat, 7 to 10 minutes, until the carrots are tender. Shake the pot frequently so the carrots don't stick and burn. You'll know they're done when the pan gets dry. Catch them just as this happens; a dry pot will enable the sugar to truly caramelize but if you wait too long they will blacken. Transfer to a warm bowl.

Khmer-Style Flank Steak
with Asian Greens and Gingered Squash

This is a potent combination—shrimp paste is like fish sauce on steroids. With the Asian Greens and Gingered Squash, your senses will be happily shaken awake. No need for rice—the powerful, refreshing Gingered Squash will give you all the starch you need.

Serves 4

GRILL OR PAN-FRY

1 stalk lemongrass

2 tablespoons lime juice

1 teaspoon shrimp paste

1 teaspoon Thai fish sauce (nam pla)

2 cloves garlic, crushed

1 tablespoon minced ginger

1 1/2 pounds flank steak, sirloin, or top blade steak

Olive oil for rubbing

1 to 2 tablespoons peanut oil for pan-frying

Kosher salt

1/4 cup chopped mint

1/4 cup chopped cilantro

1/4 cup chopped peanuts

Peel the tough outer layer off the lemongrass, then mince the bottom two-thirds of the stalk. Combine the lemongrass, lime juice, shrimp paste, fish sauce, garlic, and ginger in the bottom of a nonreactive baking dish. Stir to dissolve the shrimp paste and then put in the steak. Flip to coat and marinate for 1 hour on the counter or up to 24 hours in the refrigerator. Before cooking, remove the meat from the marinade, allow the meat to dry, and then rub with olive oil.

To grill, your coals should be so hot that you can comfortably hold your hand 2 inches above the grate for 3 seconds—just! (For gas grills, this means 450°F.) Put the oiled steak on the hottest part of the grill and sear for 3 to 5 minutes on each side over intense heat. That should be all the cooking it needs; if it needs a bit more, move it over lower heat and cook at most 2 to 5 minutes more—it should always be rare! **To pan-fry,** heat the peanut oil in a heavy pan until it's very hot—almost smoking. Sear the steak for 3 minutes on each side over high heat before turning down the burner. If your steak needs a bit more time, cook over moderate heat for at most 2 to 5 minutes more, turning often as it browns.

However you cook your steak, check for doneness often, using the finger-poke or the nick-and-peek method (see page 19). Salt your steak before resting it in a warming oven (170°F) or on a warm plate under a loose tent of foil for 5 minutes.

Thinly slice the meat and then sprinkle on the mint, cilantro, and peanuts. Serve on a large platter with the Asian Greens and Gingered Squash.

Asian Greens

Experiment with different leafy vegetables. Broccoli rabe will work here, as will Napa cabbage, bok choy, Savoy cabbage, and the always pretty Swiss chard. Don't ignore beet greens, turnip greens, collard greens, or kohlrabi, all of which need longer cooking but have heft and flavor.

6 cups greens, coarsely chopped (bok choy, Swiss chard, mustard greens, broccoli rabe, kale, spinach, or virtually any other leafy green)

2 tablespoons peanut oil

2 tablespoon grated fresh ginger

3 cloves garlic, peeled and crushed with the side of a knife

2 tablespoons dark soy sauce

1/2 cup chicken stock (page 26) or water

Sriracha sauce (optional)

Rinse the greens as needed; the water on the leaves will help them steam. If you're cooking mature mustard greens, kale, or any other leaf with a hefty stalk, be sure to begin by slicing the leaf off the stem. This is easier than it sounds. Just hold each giant leaf and with a long, sharp knife slice along the stem on each side. Finally, chop the greens.

Heat your wok over the hottest burner on high. When the wok itself is hot, add the oil, then the ginger, garlic, and heavy greens (kale, mature mustard, broccoli rabe, turnip greens, or beet greens). Watch for spattering if the greens are wet. Toss to coat with oil. After the leaves have wilted, you'll need to judge their toughness and decide how long they need to cook. Add the soy sauce along with the stock and let the greens cook for 5 minutes or so, tossing and stirring constantly. Taste. When they are close to done, add any greens that need to just wilt (baby bok choy, baby spinach). Cook until just tender. Taste for seasoning and add additional soy sauce or a squirt of Sriracha as needed.

Gingered Squash

1 acorn squash or other sweet squash such as butternut, kabocha, or delicata

Thumb-size piece fresh ginger

1 teaspoon salt

1 tablespoon very good olive oil

Cut the squash into manageable chunks and steam, or roast wrapped in foil at 350°F for 30 to 40 minutes, or until tender. Allow the squash to cool while you peel the ginger. Make sure it's fresh—not wrinkled or soft. After peeling, smash it with the side of a knife to break down the fibers, and then use a microplane or a box grater to shred it.

Once the squash is cool, cut away the skin (you can eat the skin of the delicata variety, if you like) and put the flesh in a food processor. If you don't have one, you can press it through a sieve—it just takes some doing. You should have about 2 cups. Add the ginger, salt, and olive oil. Process thoroughly to get rid of any strings or grainy texture.

Reheat gently when you're ready to serve.

Mixed Wok:
Mustard Greens, Carrots, Red Bell Pepper, and Shredded Szechuan Pepper–Rubbed Blade Steak

Szechuan pepper is an exotic-tasting little blossom that gives this simple, weekday wok dish a spicy, citrusy edge. Use vegetables that are in season. Whatever you like will work because the defining flavor comes from the peppers, soy sauce, and chili paste. This is a good choice for a winter day when May's peas, July's string beans, and August's tomatoes are long gone. Serve with Jasmine Rice (page 165).

Serves 4

WOK

1 pound top blade steak, flank steak, or skirt steak, thinly sliced, 2 to 3 inches long

2 tablespoons dark soy sauce

1 tablespoon sambal oelek (ground fresh chili paste)

1 tablespoon dried Szechuan pepper, ground

3 tablespoons peanut or vegetable oil

1 teaspoon dry mustard (I like Ridley's Gunpowder Mustard, or use a Chinese mustard)

3 cloves garlic, sliced

1 red onion, peeled and thinly sliced

1 cup mushrooms (shiitake, cremini, or oyster)

1 bunch mustard or other leafy greens, coarsely chopped (2 cups or so)

1/2 teaspoon kosher salt

1 orange or red bell pepper, thinly sliced and roughly cut into 2-inch pieces

5 carrots, peeled and grated (2 cups)

In a flat dish, combine the sliced meat with the soy sauce, sambal oelek, and ground Szechuan pepper. Let it marinate for 1 hour on the counter or up to 24 hours in the refrigerator.

Heat the wok on the highest heat. Add 2 tablespoons of the peanut oil once the wok is hot. When the oil begins to swirl and threaten to smoke, toss in half of the meat chunks. Move the meat around in the wok with a wooden spoon. Keep the heat very high and spread the meat up the sides of the wok. You don't want it to crowd together and steam. The meat should be done in 3 to 5 minutes, depending on how hot your stove is. Remove it, leaving behind the oil and juices. Transfer to a warming oven (170°F) to rest while you cook the second batch, adding the remaining 1 tablespoon of peanut oil if needed. Once the second batch is cooked, crack your oven door and turn off the oven. This will keep it warm without overcooking it.

Add any remaining marinade to the wok. Heat. Add the dry mustard, garlic, onion, mushrooms, and mustard greens. Toss and add the salt. Cook for 5 minutes before adding the pepper and carrots. Cook for another 3 to 5 minutes. Taste for seasoning; the vegetables should still hold their shape.

Put a mound of hot jasmine rice in the center of a warm platter, surround with the vegetables, and then top with the cooked meat. Pour any remaining juices from the wok on top. Sriracha, mustard sauce, and soy sauce are always welcome on the table.

Bombay Filet
with Mint-Cucumber Raita and Saffron Rice

This steak is a distant nod to the intriguing food of the Indian subcontinent, combining a spicy rub with the famously cooling raita and plenty of Saffron Rice. Evocative of Indian colors from saris to the Indian flag, this rice glistens yellow-orange and tastes of the Orient. Try it with a cold bottle of Indian Pale Ale (IPA)—high in alcohol and made with lots of hops, these beers are crisp with a bitter finish.

Serves 4

GRILL OR PAN-FRY

SPICE PASTE

1/2 teaspoon whole cardamom

1/2 teaspoon whole cumin seeds

1/2 teaspoon mustard seeds

2 teaspoons hot pepper flakes

1/2 teaspoon raw sugar (see page 29)

1 teaspoon kosher salt

Generous grind of black pepper

1 tablespoon olive oil

4 filets, roughly 1/2 pound each

1 to 2 tablespoons peanut oil for pan-frying

To make the spice paste, toast the cardamom, cumin, and mustard seeds in a small cast-iron pan until they are just fragrant. Pour the hot seeds into a mortar and add the pepper flakes, sugar, salt, and pepper. Use the pestle to grind the larger seeds. Be sure to break up the cardamom. Add the olive oil and mix.

Coat the steaks with the spice mixture and set them aside on the counter, loosely covered, to come to room temperature.

To grill, your coals should be so hot that you can comfortably hold your hand 2 inches above the grate for 3 seconds—just! (For gas grills, this means 450°F.) Put the oiled steaks on the hottest part of the grill and sear for 3 to 5 minutes on each side before you begin to fuss over them. That means moving the steaks to a cooler part of the grill and cooking for an additional 6 to 10 minutes over moderate heat, flipping, poking, and watching as you work toward crispy-brown perfection.

To pan-fry, heat the peanut oil in a heavy pan until it's very hot—almost smoking. Sear the steaks for 3 minutes on each side over high heat before turning down the burner. Cook over moderate heat for an additional 6 to 10 minutes, turning the steaks every few minutes as they slowly brown. If your house is filling with smoke, you can finish the meat by putting it, pan and all, in a 400°F oven.

However you cook your steaks, check for doneness often, using the finger-poke method, an instant-read thermometer (120° to 130°F for rare to medium-rare), or the nick-and-peek method (see page 19). Rest the steaks in a warming oven (170°F) or on a warm plate under a loose tent of foil for 5 minutes.

To serve, portion out the steak on the plates, adding a scoop of rice to each and a generous dollop of the raita tucked up next to the meat.

Mint-Cucumber Raita

1 teaspoon cumin seeds

1/2 teaspoon cayenne pepper

1/2 teaspoon kosher salt

1/2 teaspoon freshly ground pepper

1 cup plain, whole-milk Greek yogurt (Fage is the best)

Zest and juice of 1/2 lemon

3 tablespoons chopped fresh mint leaves

1/2 seedless European cucumber, chopped (1 cup)

Toast the cumin seeds in a cast-iron pan until fragrant. Remove the seeds and grind with a mortar and pestle or a spice mill. In a small bowl, combine the cumin, cayenne, salt, and pepper. Add the yogurt and beat, loosening the yogurt so it's smooth. Add the lemon zest and juice, mint leaves, and cucumber, mix thoroughly, and refrigerate until needed.

Saffron Rice

Look for Kashmiri saffron, which is not the same as the Spanish saffron that's used in paella. The best of this, the stamen of the purple crocus, is called mogra zafran.

3 tablespoons butter

1 yellow onion, coarsely chopped

2 teaspoons saffron threads

2 teaspoons kosher salt

2 cups basmati rice

4 cups chicken stock (page 26)

Melt the butter in a heavy saucepan. Add the chopped onion and cook over medium heat until soft, about 5 minutes. Add the saffron, salt, and rice and stir to coat the rice with the butter and disperse the saffron. Add the stock and cover. Cook until the stock has evaporated and the rice is tender, 15 to 20 minutes.

Pantry

CHILI PASTE (SAMBAL OELEK)

Made by Huy Fong, the same company that makes Sriracha. If you can't find it in a store, go to www.huyfong.com.

DRY-AGED PRIME BEEF

You can order dry-aged, prime-grade steaks from New York's Lobel's. Go to www.lobels.com. Another source is Chicago's famous Allen Brothers, at www.allenbrothers.com. For dry-aged, grass-fed steak, see the entry for grass-fed beef below.

FERMENTED BEAN PASTE

I love the earthy flavor of this stuff, and it adds real complexity to Chinese food. Most grocery stores carry it. Better brands can be found in Asian groceries. The ingredients should simply read "beans and salt."

FISH SAUCE

Look for real Thai fish sauce (nam pla). Any Asian grocery will carry it. The style and taste varies from country to country—Vietnamese fish sauce will taste different than Thai fish sauce. I like Three Crabs, but Tra Chang is also good and popular. The Thai supermarket at www.importfood.com is one source for both.

GRASS-FED BEEF

Niman Ranch, one of the first producers of natural meat, is an industry leader: www.nimanranch.com. Laura's Lean Beef is another source: www.laurasleanbeef.com. Whole Foods stores carry beef raised without added growth hormones or antibiotics. For meat from cattle *never* fed grain, order from La Cense Beef: www.lacensebeef.com. Finally, Montana Legend is the brand name for a group of ranchers who sell dry-aged, grass-fed steaks: www.montanalegend.com.

HOT SAUCE

For Latin food, you can buy Lottie's by mail from the owner, Jackie Health, in Katy, Texas. Call and talk to her directly (she answers the phone and takes the orders) at 866-246-5685 or go to www.lottiesislandflavours.com. Marie Sharp's is great stuff and can be used with abandon because it's not as hot as Lottie's. Look for the plan Habanero sauce with the white label. Go to www.mariesharps-bz.com.

MIRIN

Japanese cooking wine made from glutinous rice, this stuff imparts an unusual, quite distinctive flavor. I'm a real fan. Any Asian grocery and many grocery stores will carry it. Look for a naturally brewed mirin—it should *not* contain corn syrup.

OLIVE OIL

I order mine from the Rare Wine Company, in Sonoma, California. Check them out at www.rarewineco.com. Another good source is Zingerman's, at www.zingermans.com, or direct from McEvoy Ranch in California at www.mcevoyranch.com. There are more and more good oils out there. Whatever you buy, store it in a nice cool spot.

PARMIGIANO-REGGIANO

Buy a chunk that's been freshly cut from the giant wheel. I think export-quality, raw-milk Parmigiano-Reggiano is the best. Do a taste test and decide for yourself. The always impressive Murray's Cheese is where I buy mine: www.murrayscheese.com. Dean & DeLuca stores also have *great* cheese: www.deandeluca.com.

RICE

The best jasmine rice comes from Thailand and has a date on the bag. The fragrance alone makes this worth a special order if you don't have an Asian grocery nearby. I've successfully bought it from the Thai supermarket online, www.importfood.com, but I'm sure there are other good sources. Wild rice is available from Grey Owl: www.greyowlwildrice.com

SALT

Buy kosher at the grocery store. It's cheap. For the pricier Maldon, buy it by the box at Williams-Sonoma: www.williams-sonoma.com. If you're going through it by the case, get it from Salt Traders: www.salttraders.com.

SHRIMP PASTE AND DRIED SHRIMP

Both items are wonderfully smelly and salty. Each 4-ounce package of dried shrimp contains lots of shrimp since they are only about the size of a thumbnail. Shrimp paste is a bit more concentrated and can be bought from the same sources. Look for packages of the shrimp in Asian groceries or online. I like the Thai Supermarket online: www.importfood.com.

SOY SAUCE

Ranging from cheap and thin to heady and potent, the quality of soy sauce varies as much as the quality of balsamic vinegar—which is to say a lot. I use Pearl River Bridge brand; it can be found in any Chinese grocery for a buck or two. Substitute regular dark soy sauce or tamari if you don't have any, or order it online from www.importfood.com.

SPICES: BLACK PEPPER AND OTHERS

For hard-to-find items, from juniper berries to the best tellicherry pepper, you may need to look beyond the grocery store. Penzy's Spices, at www.penzys.com, is one source I like. Another source is The Spice House, at www.thespicehouse.com. Try to replace old spices often—despite their hardy appearance, they lose potency, flavor, and fragrance as they age.

SRIRACHA

This is *the* essential hot sauce for Asian—or any other—food. Made by Huy Fong Foods, it's not difficult to find these days. If you don't know where to go, you can order it directly from the company at www.huyfong.com.

TUSCAN GRILL

Make sure you buy one with a bar to adjust the height—many of the ones sold online are just grills on fixed legs. For the real thing, imported from Tuscany, order it by phone from the first U.S. importer, The Gardener, in Berkeley, California (888-509-8484). You can also order it online from Sur la Table, www.surlatable.com (they call it a Beach Side Grill). Be ready to lay out $150.

WAGYU BEEF

Snake River Farms is the biggest and best-known distributor. Go to www.snakeriverfarms.com to buy a great steak from one of these pampered beasts, or look for it at butcher shops. A large distributor to restaurants and meat markets is Imperial Wagyu Beef. Famous butchers like Chicago's Allen Brothers and the New York–based Lobel's also sell Kobe-style steaks.

WOK

I bought mine at a very cool store called the Wok Shop in San Francisco. They have a huge variety and a great website: www.thewokshop.com.

Index